NATIONAL TRUST
DORSET

TEXT Rodney Legg

Colin Graham PHOTOGRAPHS

**Frontispiece: autumn leaves at Hardy's Cottage,
the birthplace in 1840 of the Wessex
novelist and poet Thomas Hardy whose
latter-day Max Gate home, where
he died in 1928, is also owned
by the National Trust.**

DORSET PUBLISHING COMPANY
KNOCK-NA-CRE, MILBORNE PORT
SHERBORNE, DORSET DT9 5HJ

WINCANTON PRESS
NATIONAL SCHOOL, NORTH STREET
WINCANTON, SOMERSET BA9 9AT

Format

THE COUNTY has been divided into five geographical areas and a section of the book is devoted to each. Larger holdings which cover hundreds and in some cases thousands of acres have then been sub-divided into manageable entries. Around Kingston Lacy, Golden Cap and in some parts of the Isle of Purbeck the properties described have contiguous boundaries. Each entry is then divided once more into its principal strands of interest, with paragraphs in chronological order about its visible history being followed by potted descriptions of the landscape. There is then a short note of how the Trust acquired ownership and at the end of each item information about the location and its access, the parking and paths. There is also a brief note of the general location at the start of each item, together with an Ordnance Survey map reference (to six figures – the first three read west to east on the map's vertical grid; the following three south to north on the horizontal lines). As an indication of the amount of walking that a property may entail we have given acreages in the contents list that follows.

In the course of preparing this book the National Trust afforded the author and photographer access to properties as they requested. However, the book was not commissioned as an official publication nor can the National Trust take any responsibility for the views expressed within it. That there are now very few to which they can take exception is due to the moderating influence of my proof reader, Reg Ward of Holwell, who was an editor for the Dimbleby Newspaper Group.

Also by Rodney Legg

Purbeck Island
A Guide to Dorset Ghosts
Ghosts of Dorset Devon and Somerset
Editor *Steep Holm – a case history in the study of ecology*
Annotator *Monumenta Britannica* with John Fowles
Exploring Ancient Wiltshire with George Osborn
Old Portland with Jean Edwards
Romans in Britain
Purbeck Walks
Old Swanage
The Dorset Walk with Ron Dacombe, Colin Graham
Stonehenge Antiquaries
Guide to Purbeck Coast and Shipwreck
Hardy Country Walks
The Steep Holm Guide
Lulworth and Tyneham Revisited
Walks in West Dorset
The Blandford Forum Guide
Dorset's War 1939-45
Cerne's Giant and Village Guide
Purbeck's Heath – claypits, nature and the oilfield
Brownsea – Dorset's fantasy island
Blackmore Vale and Cranborne Chase Walks
East Dorset Country Walks
Exploring the Heartland of Purbeck
Wincanton's Directory, 1987
Mysterious Dorset
Dorset Encyclopedic Guide
Lawrence of Arabia in Dorset

Publishing details. First published 1987. Text copyright Rodney Legg © 1987. Photographs copyright Colin Graham © 1987.

Printing credits.
Typeset by Irene Howard
at SOS, 1 Bell Street, Shaftesbury, Dorset and printed in Somerset by Wincanton Litho.

Negative assembly and platemaking have been carried out by Andrew Johnstone and Jon Alexander.

Origination and Printing

Wincanton *Litho*

The publishers' special thanks are due to **Stephen Taylor** at Wincanton Litho for organising the production of this book, and to **Richard Kingston**, the printers' machinist.

Trade sales inquiries 0963 32583 or 0963 33643.

International standard book number
[ISBN] 0 902129 75 9

Contents

East Dorset

Isle of Purbeck

Introduction

I KNOW photographers are supposed to let their cameras speak for them but I should like to break that rule and add a few words to my pictures. All the photographs were taken in 1985 (with the exception, I think, of just one: the people looking at the Cerne Giant, which I'm rather fond of) over a ten-month period that started on a bitterly cold day in February. The first pictures I took were of the Nine Barrows on Ailwood Down in Purbeck, and although there was a bright sun shining that day, I doubt if the temperature ever once rose above freezing.

I saved until last the Hardy Monument above Portesham, Thomas Hardy's birthplace at Higher Bockhampton, and one of the few things for which we can thank Cromwell, the spectacular ruins of Corfe's castle. By that time, Hardy's Cottage, as seen from Puddletown Forest, was adrift in copper discs from the surrounding beeches, and autumn storms were sweeping in across the Chesil and briefly darkening the sky over the Hardy Monument. None of this magic appears in the pictures, of course, as I didn't have a raincoat with me and therefore stayed in the car!

In between, I think I must have walked nearly every yard of the Dorset coastline and climbed every hill there is. And I can fully recommend all of them. However, I only hope the National Trust will not take its policy of tidying the cliff-top countryside too far; there's one of those very solid-looking wooden seats on Thorncombe Beacon, above Eype's Mouth, but does it really need a very solid-looking cattle-proof wooden fence all of its own? There's a photograph on page 45.

John Cripwell, the Trust's land-agent, told Rodney Legg: "We're so ashamed of it! It is in the management plan for removal."

I think the lunacy and the luck will remain with me long after much of the rest is forgotten. In the former category I place my efforts, on Kingston Lacy Press Day at the end of August, to photograph the old Bankes home on one of those dull cloudy mornings you find in late summer. And then, just as we were all packing up, the sun came out and I had to dash round and do it over again. The luck was finding on Brownsea Island's South Beach a red squirrel that stood still long enough for me to take half a dozen pictures before it disappeared into the heather clumps. Altogether, I took about 2,200 photographs and we have whittled that number, painfully, down to precisely two hundred; my thanks to Monica Parsons for her help with the selection.

Perhaps the best thing about this project was the kindness of the people I met. I spent about six days on Brownsea and was given the freedom to photograph almost anything I chose. Obviously, I must thank Alan Bromby, the National Trust warden, but I also wish to thank Mr Dutton, the manager of Brownsea Castle, who showed me the remains of Henry VIII's blockhouse in his basement and allowed me to photograph it.

I also had help and advice from Chris Thain and Kevin Cook of the Dorset Naturalists' Trust [re-named the Dorset Trust for Nature Conservation in 1986] who allowed me free range of the nature reserve. I should point out that Brownsea Castle is *not* open to the public at all, because it is leased to the John Lewis Partnership, and there are restrictions on visiting the DTNC reserve.

In addition, the Trust's voluntary wardens on Brownsea were always very helpful, but perhaps my biggest debt is to the staff in the café: thanks lads!

When work first began on this book Rodney Legg and I had a number of discussions with John Cripwell and Tom Burr, of the National Trust's Wessex Regional office at Stourhead, about the inclusion of property owned by the Trust but not open to the public. Initially, John Cripwell was against the publication of photographs of Brownsea Castle, Thomas Hardy's house at Max Gate, and privately owned businesses such as Swanage Brick and Tile Works; and there were other National Trust properties to which the public has no access.

I pointed out to him that, to the best of my knowledge, there were no modern photographs of Max Gate currently available, that Swanage Brick Works was remarkably photogenic, that no one had seen inside Brownsea Castle, that....that readers of this book would not be so crassly irresponsible as to intrude on people's private homes or businesses. Please don't let me down.

That said, I must offer my very sincere thanks to John Cripwell and Tom Burr for subsequently supporting me in every way possible. And to Mr and Mrs Jesty, who allowed me over Max Gate, I am also very grateful. Next time I see John Fowles, I must ask him why he doesn't like the place.

The Linee family, who look after Hardy's birthplace, were very friendly, very hospitable and made a number of intelligent suggestions; and I shall long remember with great pleasure the afternoon I spent at Clouds Hill with Joyce Knowles and her dogs – and a remarkable garden full of butterflies.

And then there are all those strangers who stopped and spoke to me, who passed the time of day while I was setting up my camera. On one afternoon alone I learnt how to commit suicide at the White Nothe, and was given a marvellous description of Llewelyn Powys's bed. And there was the young man who, on another hot afternoon, discussed composition with me as we considered various ways of photographing White Mill Bridge at Sturminster Marshall. Thank you all.

For those who find technical details interesting, all the photographs (except the aforementioned Cerne Giant one) were taken on 35mm cameras using Kodak Technical Pan Film 2415 developed in Pota supplied by Speedibrews of Pyrford near Woking; and Pota *will* keep for three months, despite what they tell you. The prints were made on Kentmere paper. And most of the shots were of at least one second's duration – which meant I had to carry a tripod everywhere.

Finally, I should like to dedicate the photographs: to Jennie Duley, to John Pitfield, and to my brother Ian Graham – and to my cats Piggy and Carol, who died in 1985. All good friends!

Colin Graham – Sydney.
25 December 1985.

RODNEY LEGG, the author, has introduced a handful of Colin Graham's other pictures to illustrate points in the text, and added contemporary material on Thomas Hardy, T.E. Lawrence, and the Tolpuddle Martyrs – bringing the total number of photographs to 208. He has also added a short supplementary introduction:

It would be wishful thinking for the writer to imagine that in this kind of book the text is other than an irrelevancy.

As one who delights in historical niceties I'll take issue with Colin Graham's suggestion that we have little but Corfe Castle for which to thank Cromwell's men. The English Civil War started in "the year of discoveries", 1642, and yielded the intellectual climate that gave birth to science and knowledge in northern Europe. Newton was free to explain, "A man may imagine things that are false, but he can only understand things that are true." England was learning its way out of the Middle Ages.

I have nothing much else to add to Colin's words, apart that is to endorse his final paragraph. They were also my friends – particularly Piggy, who sat on my lap as much of this was typed, and John who came with me to explore many of the properties.

That there is a National Trust Dorset on a scale suitable for a book is due to the ultimate whim of Ralph Bankes. As befits true-born Dorset gentry he always did as he pleased and in the end it pleased him to think of the nation rather than an individual as his heir.

At the time he made up his mind the general public was showing faith in the National Trust and making it something in Dorset by enthusiastically backing its Enterprise Neptune appeal. Since the mid-1960s, during the time in which I have been boring people with such things, the Trust estates in Dorset have mushroomed from something that would have disappointed an average farmer into what is now the county's premier landholding of more than twenty thousand acres – an area of thirty-two square miles – with some of the finest countryside in these islands.

Rodney Legg
24 August 1986.

Section 1

Survey of **National Trust properties** in **West Dorset**

National Trust West Dorset is concentrated on the coast and the high ground, and includes just about all the major summits - such as Coney's Castle (above, left), and Lambert's Castle Hill (above, right), and seaward to Golden Cap (below, left). Between them the countryside is in places caught in a pastoral time-warp; as at Norchard Farm (below, right).

Black Ven: temporarily dormant landslip.

BLACK VEN
immediately west of Charmouth   *SY 356 933*

Old Lyme Road: The former main coach-road westward to Lyme Regis from the top end of Charmouth now drops into a chasm just beyond Cliff House. The road was carried off by landslips and the area is known as the Devil's Bellows. An alternative route along the cliff-edge, from Old Lyme Hill and Foxley Ridge, suffered the same fate and became part of the undercliff in 1969.

The Devil's Bellows: The history of this fast moving cliff-side has been shaped by the mudslides of the Devil's Bellows. The notable landslips of the twentieth century were in the 1920s, 1938, 1957-58 and 1969-70. One witness to the events of 1958 watched trees marching down the cliff on the crest of a mountain of debris that slid out into the sea.

The name: Ven is from 'fen', the Old English for a bog. Initial 'f' sounds were pronounced as 'v' in the Dorset dialect.

Landscape: This clifftop and undercliff, from 477 feet to sea level, forms the most active landslip in Britain. In 1969 the cliff slid two hundred yards out to sea but these mudflows have since hardened and by 1986 were half eroded by the waves.
    The geophysical cause of all this activity is the water from the clifftop

ground level, of chert gravels and upper greensand, which permeates to the gault clays which overlie the ammonite beds – reducing the clays to a great ooze of mud.   In between times of slippages the plant life recovers.

Landform geologists study this consolidation which is particularly interesting because of the great tongues of mud that change the tideline.   A small bay has developed between them.   The cliffs are leased by the National Trust to the Dorset Trust for Nature Conservation.

Trust ownership: 69 acres; 62 acres being bought with Enterprise Neptune funds, 1966-68, and the remainder being a legacy from Miss E.F.R. Nicholls and Miss E.B.I. Nicholls, 1973.

Location and access: Car-parks are near the sea in Charmouth, which is a coastal village on the A35 between Lyme Regis and Bridport.   Black Ven is immediately south-west of what's left of the Old Lyme Road at the top (west) end of Charmouth.   It is only a hundred feet from the nearest buildings in Higher Sea Lane.   In 1920 the cliff was twice that distance away.

Drainage schemes may have halted the slippage from above but in parts the undercliff is still moving.   It is dangerous to explore a mudflow, so restrict your curiosity to looking down from one of the viewpoints.

BURTON CLIFF, FRESHWATER and SOUTHOVER
at Burton Bradstock   *SY 483 893*

Smugglers' beacon: William Crowe's poem *Lewesdon Hill,* of 1788, contains an allusion to "Burton, and thy lofty cliff, where oft the nightly blaze is kindled". A footnote to the first edition explains the reference: "The cliff is among the loftiest of all upon that coast; and smugglers often take advantage of its height for the purpose related in the poem."

Landscape: Sheer 100-foot cliffs of yellow Bridport sands, above a wide beach of gritty shingle, with the hilltop pastures slanting inland and views of the Bridport countryside.   Burton Cliff is the last green hill between the caravan camps and holiday chalets.   There is a path inland from Freshwater to Burton Bradstock along the Trust's bank of the River Bride.

Trust ownership: 83½ acres.   The first forty acres were bought in 1967 with Enterprise Neptune funds and a donation from Mrs. M.B. Clark.   The other land was purchased in 1973 with a bequest from Miss M. A. Jacobsen [via CPRE] and a gift from Miss Edith M. Adlard.

Location and access: Off the B3157 Bridport to Weymouth coast road.   The Trust's car-park is approached from the Abbotsbury side of Burton Bradstock village.   Turn off opposite a thatched cottage [it has the number 93 on its door] and take the road signposted "To beach and car park".   Walk down to the beach and turn right.   The path climbs Burton Cliff and descends to the River Bride at Freshwater.

Burton Cliff: layers of soft Bridport sands, a hundred feet in height (above and opposite, with the text on the previous page), where in 1788 the smugglers were active and 'oft the nightly blaze is kindled'.

CONEY'S CASTLE
north of Charmouth   *SY 372 977*

Hill-fort: Double-banked Iron Age fort of about 400 to 300 BC with a particularly deep-cut ditch on the east side. Stout ramparts block the northern approaches and outworks were added on the southern side.   Unexcavated. Probably pre-dates Pilsdon Pen.

Name: The antiquary Charles Warne suggested in 1872 that this derives from 'Cyning', a Saxon king.   This is implausible, the obvious one being that coneys were rabbits; Norman warreners who introduced the animal to this country utilised promontories and existing enclosures, like this, to minimise the chances of escape.

Landscape: Greensand gravels and chert, formerly quarried in the north-east corner of the fort, which are now largely covered with long grass, foxgloves and scrub.   Deciduous woodland is developing in the eastern ditch but the Trust intends to bring this under control.   A conifer plantation abuts the north-west side.   On the west and east the promontory falls away steeply.
  It is over 700 feet high and has views over the Marshwood Vale.

Coney's Castle: young oaks growing between the banks.

Trust ownership: 86 acres, bought in 1975 with a legacy from Mrs K. O. Pass.

Location and access: Turn off the B3165 Lyme Regis to Crewkerne road five miles north of Uplyme – just north of where the really high pylon line, the one with 160-foot towers, crosses the road. Follow the lane to Fishpond and turn uphill in the direction of Wootton Fitzpaine. This byway climbs the spur and runs straight through the middle of the hill-fort. There is a small car-park beside the northern banks.

CROOK HILL
near Halstock   *ST 499 067*

Landscape: Though only 630 feet high, this minor hilltop lies among the attractive range of wooded slopes along the Dorset-Somerset border to the north of Beaminster. It has views over Halstock and Corscombe, and further into Dorset. In the other direction the hillside falls away and you can see Crewkerne and the Parrett valley.

**Crook Hill: the harem more or less at ease under an ash tree,
but a pair of ramshorns stand to attention.**

Trust ownership: 6 acres, given in 1965 by R.E. Trevithick.

Location and access: Turn east off the A356 Maiden Newton to Crewkerne road at Winyard's Gap. Follow this lane, towards Halstock, for almost a mile. Crook Hill rises on the north side and entails a stiff climb from the roadside.

EGGARDON HILL
north of Askerswell
SY 540 946

Hill-fort: Spectacular triple-banked Iron Age hill-fort, dating from 300 BC and given its massive multiple timbered ramparts after 50 BC. The southern half is owned by the National Trust. The north half was ploughed, across the interior and even between the banks on the north side, for crops of kale in the early 1970s; but the Trust's half is undamaged.

The visible concentration of depressions, showing the sites of pits, amounts to a grain storage capacity on a huge scale and indicates that Eggardon was the economic and administrative hub for the western Dorset chalklands.

The banks and ditches are staggered on the eastern approaches for slingstone warfare (to give the defenders' slings the advantage) and to protect the entrance. If after you arrive on the hill you turn to the left and walk the southern ramparts you will find that the central section sags down the hillside – the result of a landslip which was remedied by digging a wide ditch in the eastern part of the fallen material and reinstating the outer ditch and bank below it. Inside the earthworks, across ten acres of the southern unploughed interior, are the depressions of some 160 Iron Age pits. Those sampled by excavation were eight feet deep, with the sides cut through the clay-with-flints subsoil. They had been filled with clay. This is unusual; normally at the end of its working life a pit was used as a rubbish tip. At Eggardon they do not seem to have reached this stage. The clay was used as a bung to seal the pits and keep air and rain from the grain. The pits were therefore awaiting use when the fort was abandoned – indicating that its life was suddenly halted by the Roman invaders before the harvest had been brought in. That would have been the arrival of Vespasian's Second Legion in its three year campaign after the invasion of AD 43.

Eight circles, about thirty feet in diameter, show the sites of huts. Four Romano-British field boundaries also cross the hill, on top of at least one of the prehistoric pits. Says the Royal Commission on Historical Monuments: "With the exception of Hambledon Hill and Hod Hill this appears to be the only large hill-fort in Wessex, and probably the south of England, with extensive visible contemporary remains within it."

Octagonal sea-mark: 160 feet across, enclosed by an eighteenth century ditch and bank that cut through an ancient field bank. Reputedly constructed around a pine clump planted by the smuggler Isaac Gulliver [1745-1822] who is said to have owned the hill and wanted the trees as a navigation aid. None of the trees survives; there is but one wind-blown hawthorn on the whole of the hill.

Eggardon Hill: the view westward into the Marshwood Vale, across landslipped fortifications.

Landscape: The western escarpment of the Dorset Downs, with outstanding views across the Marshwood Vale and Lyme Bay to Dartmoor and Start Point. Downland turf with bellflowers and butterflies, including the species of the vale as well as the chalk uplands. Wall brown and marbled white mix with painted lady, brown argus, common and chalkhill blue, and four species of skipper. Higher up wheel the buzzards and hawks.

Trust ownership: 47 acres, bought from the Fry family in 1978 with various grants and donations, including a bequest from W.G. Duncombe.

Location and access: North of the A35 between Bridport and Dorchester. Turn off to Askerswell, four miles from Bridport, and take the lane uphill, under the pylon line. Eggardon is entrenched on the skyline to the left of the road.

Eggardon can also be approached from across the downs, from Maiden Newton in the north (via Wynford Eagle) and Winterbourne Abbas to the east. The second route leaves the A35 four miles west of Dorchester and continues straight ahead along the Roman road (ignore the turnings to Compton Valence), passing police radio masts and bringing you to a hilltop crossroads half a mile east of Eggardon.

Park in the layby. Walk southwards a short way, towards Bridport, and then cross the stile on the right-hand side and walk across to the earthworks. Keep to the footpath as you cross the private farmland to approach the hill-fort.

Golden Cap: from the east (above) on a balmy July day, from Seatown beach, and the view (opposite) back along from the summit. This is the highest point on the English south coast and the picture shows Seatown hamlet with Ridge Cliff beyond (centre) and then the cliffs at Burton Bradstock and the graceful curve of the Chesil Beach to Portland. Most of the nearer parts of the coastal panorama are also National Trust owned.

GOLDEN CAP
south-west of Chideock   *SY 407 923*

Claim to fame: The highest cliff on the south coast of England; 618 feet above sea level.

Cairns: Two ancient mounds, probably Bronze Age and covering burials of about 1,600 BC, about four feet high.

Triangulation pillar: Erected by the Ordnance Survey, for their instruments.

Memorial: Block of Purbeck stone with an ammonite motif and slate plaque, inscribed "Golden Cap.   Given by members of the National Trust and friends in memory of the Earl of Antrim KBE, Chairman of the National Trust from 1966 until his death in 1977. "   It was brought to the top of the cliff in 1978 in the scoop of a bulldozer.

Golden Cap: eastern undercliff and the ribbon of rocks at The Corner.

Landscape: Distinctive cliff with a name that perfectly captures its appearance. A layer of sand catches the sun.   The flat top is a horizontal mass of chert, below which the yellow band of fine sand [foxmould, which is upper greensand of the Lower Cretaceous period] contrasts with the underlying dark clays.

An extensive seascape is visible from the top, of the whole of Lyme Bay and its coastal features, and there is a breathtaking view to the waters, over landslipped debris and mudslides that have carried a ribbon of rocks – known, from right to left, as the Western Patches, The Cove, Cann Harbour and The Corner – into the sea.   It is all textbook landform geology.

Trust ownership: 26 acres, bought in 1978 in memory of Lord Antrim.

Location and access: South of the A35 between Lyme Regis and Bridport.   It is an obvious target and you have two parking choices.   The easiest walk is from Langdon Wood.   For this car-park you turn off the main road between Morcombelake and Chideock, at the top of Chideock Hill, into Muddyford Lane.   Then turn immediately left and then right into the trees.

On returning to the main road be very careful how you enter the fast traffic on this hill-top dual carriageway.

The other approach is along the coastal footpath from sea level at Seatown. For this you turn southwards in the centre of Chideock village, opposite the church, into Sea Hill Lane.

Hardown Hill: foothills of narrow lanes and scattered cottages.

HARDOWN HILL
above Morcombelake   *SY 405 945*

Barrows: Seven Bronze Age burial mounds or cairns form a skyline cemetery in the middle of the hill and date from about 2,000 BC.

Hardown Hill: furze-covered skyline burial mound.

Hardown Hill: the view west, to Lyme Regis (centre) and Charmouth (right).

Quarries: The chert deposits were worked for gravel at South Bullen, on the edge of the hill above Morcombelake, and at Johnny Vizer's Pits on the south side of the western spur overlooking Love's Lane and Verriott's Lane.

Landscape: Rising to about 650 feet, this great plateau of upper greensand and chert would be stupendous if it were nearer the sea. Instead it is landlocked, a mile from the shore behind the cliffs of Golden Cap and Stonebarrow. Its time has not yet come.

The western spur is known as The Toyte. 'Tout' was a frequent Dorset name for abrupt coastal hills.

The view seawards is partially blocked by Golden Cap, Stonebarrow and Thorncombe Beacon but inland it is uninterrupted across the Marshwood Vale and brings in the Trust's other vale-edge peaks – namely (west to east) Coney's Castle, Lambert's Castle Hill, Pilsdon Pen, Lewesdon Hill and Eggardon Hill.

Trust ownership: 25 acres, given by Mrs Angela Scott-Nicholson in 1967.

Location and access: Hardown Hill overlooks the A35 Lyme Regis to Bridport road at Morcombelake. It is ascended by several steep footpaths. These lead from the east of the village at Highbullen and Highlands, and from mid-village at Highmead and Caddy Road, as well as Love's Lane. On the north side there are paths from Taylor's Lane and Loscombe's Well Road. The eastern face is climbed from Charleston Corner on the Ryall Road.

Lambert's Castle: Iron Age rampart overlooking the Marshwood Vale.

LAMBERT'S CASTLE HILL
north of Lyme Regis   *SY 370 986*

Hill-fort: Single-banked Iron Age hill-fort of about 400 to 300 BC with an outer ditch that is much better preserved than the rampart.   Unexcavated, but probably earlier than Pilsdon Pen.

Beacon: Mediaeval beacon site; almost certainly.

Fair and Racecourse: Annual fair held inside the fort on the Wednesday preceding John the Baptist's day [24 June] from 1709 to 1947.   The site of the Fair House is immediately inside the fort entrance, on the right–hand side, and other low earthworks mark the sites of stalls and sheep enclosures.   Horse–races were part of the fair and the racecourse was a circuit of the open hilltop south of the fort.   For a time, in the nineteenth century, a second fair was held in September.

Admiralty Telegraph Station: On the flat top of the hill-fort, east from the centre 220 metres from the entrance.   This is the site of a shutter–telegraph built in the winter of 1805–06 by George Roebuck.

The system which crossed Dorset was known as the Plymouth Line. Lookouts used telescopes to watch the next stations along the line [Toller Down to the east and Dalwood Common in the west].   Roebuck's system was built at the height of the Napoleonic wars in the months after the Battle of

Trafalgar. A warning of invasion in the West Country could have been transmitted to Whitehall in about thirty minutes – if it happened on a clear day.

In 1822 the stations were converted to a simpler semaphore system devised by Sir Home Riggs Popham. They were replaced by the Electric Telegraph in 1847.

Name: 'Lamberht' – a Saxon personal name – with 'Labirihtes Gete' being the name for the gap in the hills [as with Corfe Gate being the name of the pass at Corfe Castle].

Landscape: The hill rises to 842 feet, with views westward to Dartmoor and across the Marshwood Vale to the Chesil Beach and Portland. There is a typical common land look to the south-western parts of the hill, with unfenced roads, and patches of gorse scrub heath. The north-west slopes are heavily wooded, with the most westerly beech wood in Dorset.

Trust ownership: 167 acres, given in 1956 by Colonel A.D. Pass.

Location and access: Beside the B3165 Lyme Regis to Crewkerne road, five miles north of Uplyme to the north of where the 160-foot high pylons carry the national grid across the road.

The Trust has a car-park to the south of the hill-fort. There is also a layby beside the phone box on the northern slopes and from there you climb up through the trees.

Lewesdon Hill: its beechwoods from the south, with Brimbley Coombe Farm below.

LEWESDON HILL
near Broadwindsor

ST 437 013

Hill-fort: Small early Iron Age single-banked encampment of about 400 to 300 BC; earlier than Pilsdon Pen.

Name: 'Leuson' – Saxon personal name.

Landscape: High, rounded hill rising to about 900 feet and heavily wooded, with beech. Completely different in character from the other nearby hill, Pilsdon Pen, and hence the saying that was first recorded in 1662, "As much akin as Leuson Hill to Pilsen Pen."

Mariners used to call them the "Cow and Calf" [Lewesdon was the calf]. The hill overlooks the pastoral Marshwood Vale and inland to Devon and Somerset.

Literary associations: Inspired the poem that carries its name, *Lewesdon Hill,* a lengthy romantic movement offering of 1788 by William Crowe, the rector of Stoke Abbott. This is a brief extract:

> "Thou nameless rivulett, who from the side
> Of Lewesdon softly welling forth, doth trip
> Adown the valley, wandering sportively.
> Alas, how soon thy little course will end !
> How soon thy infant stream shall lose itself
> In the salt mass of waters, ere it goes.
> No name or greatness.
> Yet it flows along
> Untainted with the commerce of the world,
> Or passing by the noisy haunts of men;
> But through sequestered meads, a little spate,
> Winds frequently, and in its wanton path,
> May cheer some droopy flowers, or minister
> Of its cool water to the thirsty lamb:
> Then falls into the ravenous sea, as pure
> As when it issued from its native hill."

Mineral waters: The water from these hills has been bottled and sold under the name "Lewesdon Spring". In 1985 it was the brand available in the House of Commons cafeterias.

Trust ownership: 27 acres, given in 1943 by Colonel R.P.J. Mitchell.

Location and access: On the west side of the B3162 Bridport to Broadwindsor road, a mile south-east of Broadwindsor. It is a half mile walk and climb westward along a track from the cottages at Stoke Knap.

Parking here is not easy, because it is a junction on a narrow bend. It would be sensible to turn off east, and drop down into Stoke Abbott which is a mile away. Walk back to Stoke Knap and cross the main road to the double-hedged track on the opposite side.

Lewesdon Hill: on the skyline (above, centre) from the east side of Pilsdon Pen hill-fort – its profile giving rise to the west Dorset saying, 'As much akin as Lewesdon Hill to Pilsdon Pen' ... meaning completely unlike. You can compare the two upper pictures on this spread and judge for yourself.

Lewesdon Hill: contorted beech bole with a tangle of roots left airborne by a couple of centuries of soil erosion.

Pilsdon Pen: the plateau, from the south-east.

PILSDON PEN
west of Broadwindsor   *ST 414 012*

Hill-fort: Major Iron Age hill-fort with triple banks and ditches between, built
by iron-using Celtic settlers from across the Channel after 200 BC.   They
enclosed nine acres of a flat-topped spur.   Their key weapon was the sling,
firing rounded pebbles.

   This important Durotrigic fortress probably superseded the string of smaller
forts [Lambert's Castle, Coney's Castle, Lewesdon Hill] that can be seen from
its ramparts.   Excavation has revealed areas of stained soil that mark the sites of
wattle and daub huts and a spread of coarse, blackened pottery.   Gold-
smelting crucibles were the outstanding finds, together with a Romano–Celtic
temple.   It was a large building, about fifty yards square, and slingstones were
found along its foundations.

   The dig, which took place from 1963 to 1971, also uncovered evidence that
Pilsdon Pen may have been one of the native fortresses stormed by Vespasian's
Second Legion, probably towards the end of its conquest of the West, about
AD 45-46.   They found a Roman spearhead and ballista bolt.   The latter
indicates that a heavy artillery piece was hauled up the hill – which would
hardly have been done other than for an attack.

Name: Pilsdon is the name of the parish [though it quite likely takes its name from the hill] and 'Pen' is an old English word for an enclosure that held stock.

Landscape: Pilsdon Pen is a great chert plateau, with the distinction at 908 feet of being the highest point in Dorset. It has a distant view to Dartmoor and a near one of the Marshwood Vale – spread out below and fringed by Trust-owned hills – and the coastline of Lyme Bay. The seaward extremities are Portland Bill in the east and Start Point to the south-west. On the exposed hilltop the impoverished soil favours a tough flora which includes gorse and bilberries.

Trust ownership: 36 acres, bought from the Pinney family in 1979 with money bequeathed by Miss P.M. Hardcastle and Miss E.V.A. Compton in memory of Leslie Spencer Compton.

Location and access: Dominates the B3164 between Broadwindsor and Birdsmoorgate, where the B3164 joins the B3165 road (Lyme Regis to Crewkerne). Parking is at the foot of the hill in a layby beside the turning to Pilsdon. Cross the road to the stile. It is a stiff climb to the top.

Pilsdon Pen: looking southwards, towards the sea, along the inner rampart on the west side of the Iron Age hill-fort. This exposed hilltop, at 908 feet, is the highest point in the county of Dorset.

Saint Wite's Well: modern kerb to an ancient shrine.

SAINT WITE'S WELL and SHIP FARM
south of Morcombelake

SY 400 940

Saint Wite's Well (SY 399 937):   Lying by the track at the foot of the eastern slope of Chardown Hill, this sacred well is a mile from the martyr's shrine, which is in Whitchurch Canonicorum parish church.

It is known as "Saint Vita's Well" to the people of Morcombelake and was an "eye-well" that provided "a sovereign cure for sore eyes" if the dousing took place in the first light of a new day; perhaps the time of day contributed to the general shock.   Bent pins were dropped in the well-head with the request: "Holy well, holy well, take my gift and cast a spell."

Thomas Gerard, writing in the 1620s, says Saint Wite "lived in prayer and contemplation" near Whitchurch, "not far off in the side of a hill", which perfectly describes this spot.   Local people are quite certain, and for years the well-site has been shown by the Ordnance Survey in the gothic type that depicts antiquity.   "The Saint's Well" it says on the current 6-inch map.

In the mid–1980s, before restoring a stone kerb to the site of the well, the National Trust would not admit that the spring was a holy well.   "There is no absolute proof," they said, and passed on the verdict of the county archaeologist that it is merely an ancient spring.   Nevertheless, warden Toby Eaton was prepared to compromise by calling it the "Saint's Well" – which is where the Ordnance Survey arrived many years ago, and which begs an inevitable question.   Which saint?

Local people had no doubt and knew the periwinkles on Stonebarrow Hill as "Saint Candida's Eyes".   Candida is a latinisation of Saint Wite's name and the plant-name also perpetuates the connection with eye-cures.   Christine Waters is also without any doubts and her booklet entitled *Who was Saint Wite?* [sold in Whitchurch Canonicorum church] calls it Saint Wite's Well and says that the side of the field around the well-head was allowed to become smothered in brushwood in the 1930s, to prevent cattle stumbling in, and the spring piped into a trough. The old kerbing has disappeared and the modern trough is a replacement.

About Saint Wite: The Norman latinisation to Candida was on the wrongful assumption that "Wite" meant "White". Wite is thought to have been with the team of fifty who went with Saint Boniface of Crediton on his final mission to Germany. It ended with a massacre at Dockum, near Utrecht, on 5 June 755.

Boniface's remains were carried to the abbey at Fulda but it is unlikely that those of his minions could have been brought back to Britain for burial. Few of our war dead were returned in the twentieth century and the freight problems of the Dark Ages must have been inordinately prohibitive.

Anyway, Archbishop Cuthbert of Canterbury decreed to a shocked emergency synod that "Saint Boniface and his cohort should have their martyrdoms celebrated annually throughout the Church in England at Whitsuntide." This quote has since been distorted to read the "Church of England" – what he meant was the Church of Rome in England.

That was the time for the yearly dedicatory festival at Whitchurch Canonicorum, until it was changed in the reign of Henry VIII, though Whitsun must have seemed as good a time as any to celebrate Saint "White".

Local tradition does not go along with the Boniface connection and insists that Wite was killed by Danish pirates in a raid on Charmouth in the ninth century. Historians have stated this raid to be an absolute fact but the present author has uncovered no contemporary evidence.

The only certainty in all this is that Wite's thirteenth century tomb at Whitchurch Canonicorum is one of only two martyrs' shrines that have survived intact in the whole of England. Its top is a stone chest of Purbeck marble, with three egg-shaped openings below, into which even today are placed pathetic offerings of money and cards and notes begging her intercession on behalf of the sick. The chest was damaged by subsidence in the winter of 1899 and in April 1900 repairs were carried out. Inside, on its edge at the north side, there was an oblong lead reliquary, twenty-nine inches long, inscribed "+HIC.REQUESCT.RELIQUE.SCE.WITE" [Here rest the relics of Saint Wite]. There were signs that it may have been opened in the sixteenth century. At the top was a thigh-bone, fourteen inches in length, and the bones were described as "the remains of a small woman, apparently about forty years old".

About 1910 some relics were found in Lambeth Palace that included one labelled "the thigh-bone of Saint Candida" (her Latin name) which validated an old local tradition that one of the thigh-bones was missing from the tomb. It was the custom, when an archbishop translated a saint's bones, for him to take one with him.

Landscape: The well is set in the small fields of a hillside dairy farm a short distance from the busy coast road at Morcombelake.

Trust ownership: 39 acres, bought in 1969 with money left to the Trust by R.I. Gunn.

Location and access: Ship Farm lies off the A35 between Lyme Regis and Bridport, at the west end of Morcombelake.   It is on the seaward side of the road.   There is a lane past the farm that climbs Chardown Hill to the Trust's parking and picnic area on the top.   This green lane has no vehicular right of way and is only a footpath.   Cars are prohibited, so to reach the Stonebarrow Hill car-park you have to approach from the other side, up Stonebarrow Lane from just east of the river bridge at Charmouth [the old course of the A35 once the by-pass is completed].   Park at the far end of the car-park by the pine trees.   Take the green lane marked "Morcombelake".

Walk downhill for half a mile to the track on the right just before you reach Ship Farm.   The well is about two hundred yards along this track [midway to the bungalow known as Coldharbour] in the field to the right.

Ridge Cliff: from the beach at Seatown.

SEATOWN, RIDGE CLIFF and WEST CLIFF
seaward of Chideock   *SY 422 920*

First landing of Monmouth's rebels: In the morning of 11 June 1685, two men were rowed on to Seatown beach – an English gentleman, Thomas Dare, and a fiery Scot, Andrew Lord Fletcher.   The latter was second-in-command of the Duke of Monmouth's cavalry and they slipped into Dorset to organise their

Seatown and Ridge Cliff: from the slopes of Golden Cap.

chief's imminent attempt at seizing the throne from his uncle, James II.

Their exploits were to be fully in line with the failure of the whole expedition. Fletcher tried to commandeer Dare's horse. The Englishman refused and raised his whip and was shot by Fletcher through the head.

The volunteers who witnessed the incident wanted Fletcher strung up but he was smuggled back on board ship and escaped to Spain. Nevertheless these were two disastrous own-goals for Monmouth's side. Fletcher could have been invaluable; an aggressive Scot was just what Monmouth lacked at the head of his cavalry for the skirmish at Bridport and the Battle of Sedgemoor. And Thomas Dare had the finance.

Smugglers: As much as any in Dorset, because of homes near the beach and the absence of any nearby town or Coast Guard presence, the fishermen of Seatown had a reputation for being the most successful smugglers along this coast.

It was their achievement that brandy was kept below four shillings a bottle in Yeovil for almost the whole of the eighteenth century.

Landscape: Undercliff and cliff-sides rise from the little anchorage of Seatown where the River Winniford trickles through a high pebble bank into Lyme Bay.

These cliffs are of crumbling and slipping blue lias clays and the beach is stony. Dominating everything is the massive Golden Cap clifftop [*which has its own entry*]; 618 feet higher than the beach and a mile away. West Cliff is unstable and landslipped. Ridge Cliff, on the east side of Seatown, is a tilted pasture rising to 350 feet. It drops sheer into the sea at East Ebb and the Magging Stone.

Trust ownership: 170 acres, the greater part bought in 1966 through an anonymous donation to Enterprise Neptune. The remaining 25 acres were added from general Neptune funds in 1974.

Location and access: Off the A35 between Bridport and Lyme Regis. Turn south at Chideock. Sea Hill Lane, opposite the church, terminates in a car-park beside the sea at Seatown. On each side the coastal footpath leads upwards into the Trust's lands.

THE SPITTLES
immediately east of Lyme Regis   *SY 350 930*

The Lyme Volcano: This was the tag given to the 1908 spontaneous combustion that started in the oily shales that overlie the blue lias boulders. The cliff smouldered away for several years, though its later life was said to have been prolonged by cartloads of coal donated by Lyme traders who did not

The Spittles: the old Lyme to Charmouth road provides a metalled footpath at the edge of this landslipped cliff which is now a nature reserve managed by the Dorset Trust for Nature Conservation.

The Spittles: an active mudflow (centre), runs down to the sea. This view is eastwards, towards Charmouth.

wish to lose their tourist attraction. The Trust owns another Burning Cliff, at Ringstead Bay, which is listed with the Central Dorset properties.

The name: Spittles is among the most descriptive names on the Dorset coast, the mudflows appearing as if they were spat out from the cliff. Disappointingly, the researched origin of the name is that the middle English 'spitel' was land on which a hospital was built – unlikely in this case – or land owned by a hospital.

Landscape: Cracking meadows and landslipped undercliff. The eastern end of the Spittles, next to Black Ven, was carried across the Canary Ledges and into the sea by mudflows in 1959 and 1969-70.

Other parts of the cliff have edged towards the sea in recent years, the slippage being caused by rainfall seeping down through the chert and greensand top layers which then slide off the underlying liassic clays. The area is leased by the National Trust to the Dorset Trust for Nature Conservation.

Trust ownership: 126 acres, bought with Enterprise Neptune funds in 1974.

Location and access: Park in Lyme Regis. Where the South-West coast footpath leaves the town on the east side, opposite the cemetery, it skirts above The Spittles. This, and any path in the cliff area, is liable to diversion or closure in the event of further landslips. Do not venture on to an active mudflow.

Stanton St Gabriel: green and cottage at the heart of the best traditionally-farmed landscape in Dorset.

STANTON ST GABRIEL, SHEDBUSH FARM, NORCHARD FARM, FILCOMBE FARM and LANGDON HILL
south of Morcombelake   *SY 401 924*

St Gabriel's chapel (SY 402 924):   Thirteenth century lias–stone ruin. Services were last held before 1800.   After the French wars the church was used as "a receiving house for smugglers' kegs of brandy".

Stanton St Gabriel (SY 400 924):   There are few buildings now but in 1650 twenty-three families were living around the green. The surviving thatched cottages are let by the Trust for self–catering holidays.   "Please remember to feed the badger" is on the list of instructions.

Shedbush Farm (SY 405 934):   Typical yellow–stone and thatch buildings of a small west Dorset dairy farm, forming an unusually complete collection and dating from 1700.

Beach access, on foot: From Stanton St Gabriel, down the valley to St Gabriel's Mouth.   Descend a steep gully.   Offshore is St Gabriel's Ledge.   You venture down there at your own risk.

Stanton St Gabriel: Golden Cap behind.

Landscape: Small fields and dense hedgerows, tall and overhanging, of a nineteenth century mixed farming landscape that has been preserved by the Trust.   These are lush meadows on a clay soil.   Some of the hedges reached house–height in 1985 though they were then cut and laid.

Nowhere else in Dorset is unimproved pastureland still farmed on this scale.   It is a most remarkable valley, caught in a time-warp.   There are also coppices and larger pine woods, Monument Copse and Langdon Hill, which are under-stood with holly.   The views are of Lyme Regis and Golden Cap, which dominates the scene and has its own entry.

Trust ownership: 505 acres, bought in 1967-72 with Enterprise Neptune funds and legacies from Miss Jessie McNab, R.I. Gunn, and Miss Gwendolen Pelly.

Location and access: South of the A35 between Lyme Regis and Bridport. Seaward of Morcombelake.   Turn off the A35 between Morcombelake and Chideock, at the top of Chideock Hill, into Muddyford Lane.   Then turn immediately left and then right into the trees.   There is a car-park at the end in the wood on Langdon Hill.   Walk back along the lane and then turn left, to Stanton St Gabriel.   It is a mile walk.   Paths branch off to the farms and you can return to Langdon Hill from the cliff footpath, via Golden Cap.

On returning to the main road be very careful how you enter the fast traffic on this hill-top dual carriageway.

Stanton St Gabriel: the farm is now divided into holiday cottages, and St Gabriel's chapel (below), is in ruin.

Stanton St Gabriel: looking down on the parish and its cottages (above, near right – and below in detail) from Golden Cap.

Stonebarrow Hill: close-cropped turf beside the car-park.

STONEBARROW HILL, CAIN'S FOLLY, CHARDOWN HILL, NEWLANDS BATCH, WESTHAY FARM and UPCOT FARM
east of Charmouth   *SY 385 935*

Ancient trackway: The track across the top of Stonebarrow Hill, beside which the Trust has established a picnic area, was the main road from Charmouth to Morcombelake until it was replaced by the northern turnpike [the present A35, until completion of the Charmouth by-pass] in 1824.   It was the main Dorchester to Exeter coach road and seems to be on the course of the 'lost' Roman road between the two towns.

Wartime radar station (SY 378 930):   On the undercliff, 150 feet below Cain's Folly cliff-edge, visible only from the top.   It slipped down the cliff in a landslip on 14 May 1942, to the surprise of the RAF crew who are reputed to have been inside it at the time, and who stepped out when it came to a halt.

Post-war radar station (SY 383 934):   At the centre of Stonebarrow Hill, behind a high security fence, relinquished by the Ministry of Defence in 1978 and used by the Trust as an information point and base for work parties.

Names: Stonebarrow must have been an ancient cairn, but it has disappeared – in all probability in order to fill ruts in the road.

Cain's Folly is recorded as the name of the landslipped wood, but sounds as if it must have been coined originally for a building that went the same way.

Westhay Farm is Old English, meaning simply 'west enclosure', and Upcot is just as easy – 'upper house'.

Upcot Farm: Chardown Hill behind.

Landscape: Chert-topped plateau of upper greensand, prone to gorse scrub on the south side but heavily wooded on the damper northern slopes [Newlands Batch].   The seaward end of this mile-long 500–foot high ridge is known as Cain's Folly, the name being last applied to a beech clump that went over the cliff in 1942.

Here the wartime radar station lies tilting in a trough but other parts of the thousand–foot wide undercliff came down in 1877.   The sliding gault clays brought with them a hundred and fifty feet of upper greensand and chert, which comprise the walkable top of the headland.   This cliff edge has receded by four hundred feet since the 1860s but the loss of undercliff into the sea is at a much slower rate, of just over a hundred feet in the same period.

The sea views are to Start Point and Golden Cap.   Inland there are the Trust-owned peaks of Lambert's Castle, Pilsdon Pen and Lewesdon, with Hardown Hill nearer and to the right.   The Trust's immediately adjacent lands extend along the ridge to Chardown Hill and downhill to the small pastures around Westhay and Upcot farms.

Trust ownership: 771 acres, of which 274 acres at Stonebarrow Hill and Westhay Farm were the starting point for the Trust's Golden Cap estate, being given in 1961 in memory of Oliver Morland.   The remainder was acquired in 1966 with Enterprise Neptune funds, except for 61 acres which were added in 1978–81 through a variety of appeal funds and a legacy from Miss S.W. St Paul.

Westhay Farm: Stonebarrow Hill behind, with Cain's Folly at its left-hand end.

Stonebarrow Hill: ex-radar station, now a National Trust wardening base and shop.

Cain's Folly: aspects of coastal erosion, past (below, the wartime radar station), present, and future (cliff edge opposite, about to descend).

Location and access: Stonebarrow is the hill immediately east of Charmouth, to the south of the A35 between Lyme Regis and Bridport.   It is climbed by Stonebarrow Lane, which starts beside the Newlands Hotel, but drive slowly and cautiously.   It is narrow, winding and dangerous.   Sound your horn at corners and prepare to encounter walkers trapped between cars or obscured by the high banks.   At the top you cross a cattle-grid into the Trust's picnic area car-park.

Stonebarrow Hill: mist rising off the sea.

THORNCOMBE BEACON, DOWNHOUSE FARM
and DOGHOUSE HILL
west of Bridport   *SY 440 915*

Barrows (SY 436 916 *and* SY 437 917):   Three Bronze Age burial mounds, two of them on the Trust's lands, lie between Down House and Thorncombe Beacon.

Beacon (SY 435 914):   There is a mediaeval and Elizabethan beacon site, as its name suggests, on the Thorncombe Beacon clifftop.

Pillbox [site of]:   A World War Two underground shelter on Thorncombe Beacon, either part of the anti-invasion defences or connected with the secret

Thorncombe Beacon, in the direction of: a view in the mist, westward from Eype beach.
Thorncombe Beacon: fenced wooden seat on the summit.

radar stations that operated along this coast, was regarded as an eyesore and blown up by the Trust. Toads used to live in it.

Landscape: Expansive vistas of Lyme Bay and the Chesil Beach from Thorncombe Beacon which is a 508-foot high chert-topped plateau. It is one of the great Dorset cliffs and is particularly steep on the side facing Bridport. The Great Ebb and other ledges break the surf at its foot.

Doghouse Hill is also some climb, at 400 feet, but represents no more than the eastern foothills to Thorncombe Beacon.

Trust ownership: 230 acres. Downhouse Farm and Thorncombe Beacon were given to the Trust by R. C. Sheriff in 1966. 54 acres at Doghouse Hill were added to the holding through the Enterprise Neptune appeal in 1967.

Location and access: South of the A35 to the west of Bridport. The ascent of Thorncombe Beacon is along the coastal footpath, uphill from the east [Eype Mouth, a mile of tough climbing] or from the west [Seatown, just over a mile but not quite as steep]. Eype Mouth is reached by lanes from Bridport – turn west from South Street at the Brewery.

Seatown is reached from Chideock. Turn south off the A35 in the centre of the village, opposite the church, and drive the length of Sea Hill Lane. Take to the coastal path at the end, uphill out of the car-park.

Downhouse Farm: curious circular drinking trough at the foot of Thorncombe Beacon.

West Bexington: Labour-in-Vain Farm.

WEST BEXINGTON, LIMEKILN HILL, TULK'S HILL, LABOUR-IN-VAIN FARM and THE CHESIL BEACH
west of Abbotsbury   *SY 547 867*

Bronze Age burial mounds (westwards from SY 544 868):   Group of several well preserved round barrows strung along the skyline at Tulk's Hill, dating from about 2,000 BC in the Bronze Age.

Limekiln (SY 540 870): Limekiln Hill has the undulations of limestone quarries, into the iron-stained beds that give Abbotsbury its rich colours, and its name comes from the kiln which survives at the edge of the escarpment.   Dating from the early nineteenth century it produced building mortar and limewash. It would have been filled from the top with alternating layers of stone and wood, the slow combustion converting the rock into quicklime.

Pillboxes: In the fields and beside the beach are concrete emplacements that were the anti-invasion defences of 1940.

The name: Labour-in-Vain is one of those Dorset names that evokes an image of perpetual exhaustion for zero reward.   It is a reminder that before the days of tractors and subsidies farming was not much fun on the thin soils beside an exposed shoreline.   Nearby, in contrast, is a farm known as Peace and Plenty.

West Bexington: Limekiln Hill and (opposite) its limekiln.

Landscape: The ridge has fine views over Lyme Bay and down to the Chesil Beach, a stretch of which is in the Trust's ownership to the west of the former Abbotsbury Coastguard Station. Grain is grown between the beach and the hills but the escarpment is reserved for rough grazing and roe deer, with extensive scrubland on Tulk's Hill. Some young oaks were planted in memory of Dennis Cosgrove [1924–80], an Australian scientist who researched inositol phosphates but maintained a lifelong enthusiasm for the Dorset countryside.

Trust ownership: 262 acres. Limekiln Hill was given by Sir Ronald Milne Watson in 1964, and an additional twenty acres bought in 1965–70 with moneys from Mrs Ella Corbett. The 225 acres of Labour-in-Vain Farm came to the Trust from the Treasury in 1979, through the National Land Fund.

Location and access: The ridge is beside the B3157 Bridport to Weymouth coast road, between Swyre and Abbotsbury, and there is parking at Limekiln Hill.

At Labour-in-Vain, to the west of the old Abbotsbury Coastguard Station, the Trust owns a section of the famous Chesil Beach. This is beside the Burton Road, a public highway which runs immediately inland of the Chesil Beach from Abbotsbury Sub Tropical Gardens (first turning seaward to the west of the village) to West Bexington. It is unwise to drive along it because much of its length is rutted, covered with shingle, or otherwise hostile for vehicles. A more sensible approach is to turn south off the B3157 at Swyre to the car-park

West Bexington: Labour-in-Vain Farm and the western end of the Chesil Beach, from Tulk's Hill.

in West Bexington. Walk half a mile eastwards along the coast path. Public paths cross the fields to Labour-in-Vain and the ridge at Limekiln Hill and Tulk's Hill. Keep to the public footpaths on this tenanted farmland.

WINYARD'S GAP, CRATE'S COPPICE, PENNEY'S HILL COPPICE, WHITE HILL PLANTATION and NORTH HILL PLANTATION
above Chedington   *ST 491 061*

Memorial (ST 491 060): To the war dead of the 43rd (Wessex) Division of the Territorial Army in the campaign from Normandy to the Baltic, 1944–45. It is a replica of the memorial on Point 112 behind the D-Day beach-head at Caen and is one of a number unveiled on West Country hilltops in 1952.

Name: 'Wynheard' – a Saxon personal name. 'Gap' – the pass through the hills which has been a main road for centuries. Charles I passed through it in 1644 and, it was observed, "he rode the great horse very well".

Landscape: Dense, north-facing, woodland on the escarpment above Winyard's Gap where the road climbs a deep cutting into a lip of the Dorset Downs. This is a fine viewpoint, from 800 feet, over two distinct regions.

To the west is the valley of the River Axe (which begins as a trickle less than

Winyard's Gap: replica of the memorial on Point 112, the hill south-west of Caen, between Esquay and Eterville, which the 43rd (Wessex) Division attacked at 05.00 hours on 10 July 1944. They took the hill but were driven out of the nearby village of Maltot by a strong German counter-attack and on 11 July had to hold Point 112 against an onslaught from the 10th SS Panzer Division.

a mile from here) winding between the hills of Dorset and Somerset before slipping into Devon. Eastward is the gathering flatness that becomes the Blackmore Vale, interspersed with ripples of undistinguished hilliness that fail to compete with the solid line of the chalk escarpment.

Literary associations: 'The Three Horseshoes', as the Winyard's Gap inn was known, features in *The Clear State of the Case of Elizabeth Canning,* a rare 1752 pamphlet by Henry Fielding concerning a notorious gipsy-alibi trial. Canning may have been the victim or villain, kidnapped or prostitute. At any event she was convicted and transported. Mary Squires was either abductress or scapegoat – innocent gipsy or brothel matron. The jury thought the worse and she was sentenced to hang but this was pardoned.

Trust ownership: 16 acres, given in 1949 as a memorial to the 43rd Division.

Location and access: The A356 road from Maiden Newton to Crewkerne drops from above the 800 feet contour to only 200 feet in a two mile stretch at Chedington.

Turn towards Chedington at the Winyard's Gap inn. After the next small block of trees, beyond the public house, there is another small car-park from which a footpath leads up the hill to the memorial.

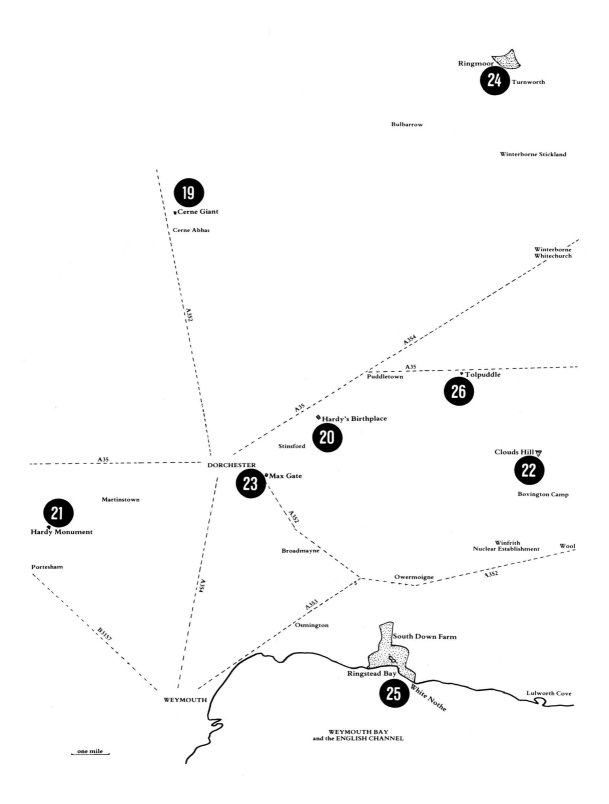

Section 2

Survey of **National Trust properties** in **Central Dorset**

NEXT PAGE, the Cerne Giant: his outstanding twentieth century portrait, from the work of Sir Flinders Petrie, published by the Royal Anthropological Institute in 1926. Its measurements were taken on the sloping ground, and if reduced to a horizontal plane (as on a map) the figure would be about ten per cent shorter. About 220 points were plotted around the Giant's outline. Petrie described his methods: 'The plan was made by stretching a line down the whole figure, and setting another line at right angles across the shoulders, and a parallel line across the legs. Standing at any required point, I held two tape measures; the zero of one was held on the long line by my wife, the zero of the other on a cross line by my son, keeping the tapes square with the lines. I then read off the two distances to the spot on the ground, and plotted it at once on squared paper.'

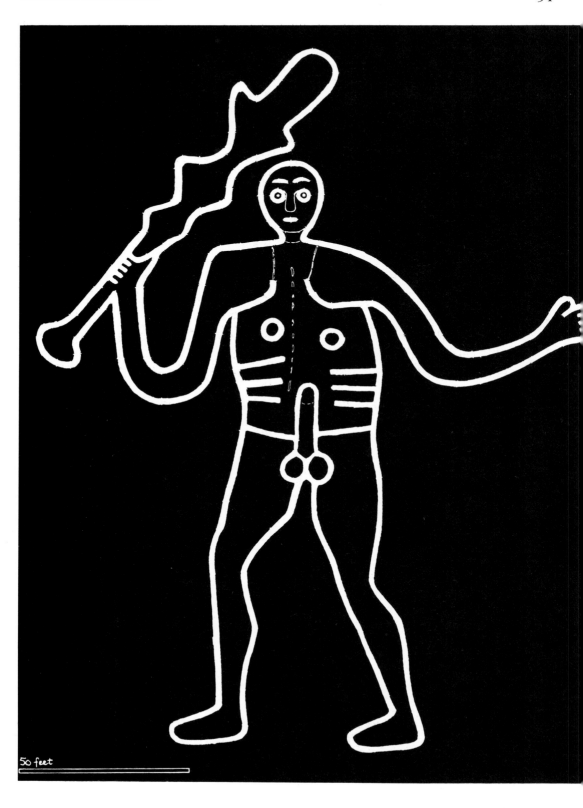

50 feet

Cerne Giant: roadside view of Britain's oldest full-frontal nude on permanent public display.

CERNE GIANT
at Cerne Abbas   *ST 666 016*

Hill-figure: One hundred and eighty feet high outline, said to be of the first century AD, of a naked man brandishing a club that is one hundred and twenty feet long.   The trenches that comprise the Giant are no more than two feet wide and are cut into the chalk of a steep hillside overlooking the Cerne valley. The figure has been frequently scoured through the ages, including the period when Cerne was a major Benedictine monastery, to prevent it disappearing under the turf.

This is either a representation of the Roman god Hercules, cut in a native style [the general archaeological opinion] or the Celtic lord of the animals, Cernunnos [the alternative viewpoint].   There was a lion's skin [if Hercules] or serpent [if Cernunnos] draped over the outstretched arm, that was rediscovered in 1979 when Yorkshire Television used a resistivity meter to detect former trenches under the grass.

The nose also survives under the ground, its long parallel sides joined with the eyes like an inverted phallus; it was common in Celtic art for the eyes and nose to be depicted as an upside-down phallus.   The Giant's penis is now twenty-two feet in length, because an early twentieth century recutting absorbed the navel into its tip and thereby extended the organ to what is a total of thirty feet if the testicles are included.   Phallic representations are common in British Celtic culture and throughout the Roman world.   For further information see my own *Cerne Giant and Village Guide* [1986].

The name: Cerne, the local river name, is of great antiquity and it is surely more than coincidence that this is the first half of the name of an important Celtic deity.   Cernunnos, according to the mediaeval Welsh *Mabinogion,* was the "lord of the wild beasts" who wielded an "iron club" and was "not smaller than two men of this world" – in other words, he was a giant.   There is evidence of other lost trenches on the Cerne hillside and these may represent accompanying animals in what was perhaps originally a frieze of Celtic figures.

Landscape: The figure is cut into the steep west-facing escarpment of Giant Hill and a block of unspoilt downland rises around it.

Trust ownership: Half acre given to the Trust in 1920 by the Pitt-Rivers family and endowed by Sir Henry Hoare in 1924.   A further area of hillside was loaned in the 1970s to make the enclosure a manageable size.

Location and access: Overlooking the valley road from Dorchester to Sherborne on the northern side of Cerne Abbas.   A public footpath skirts the Giant's enclosure.   This path runs northwards from the cemetery at the end of Abbey Street, towards the left hand end of the clump of trees and then uphill, diagonally up the steep slope.   There is no access, however, inside the fence; this is a sheep pen.

The figure is clearly visible from a layby, half a mile away beside the valley road, and in a wider panorama from Sydling Hill where the lane to Sydling St Nicholas crosses the next wave of downland.

HARDY'S COTTAGE
Higher Bockhampton, east of Dorchester   *SY 728 925*

Author's birthplace: The thatched cottage where life began for Thomas Hardy, as a frailty which the nurse thought was dying, on 2 June 1840.   This room is upstairs, above the living room, at the north end of the cottage and what became Hardy's own room is above the kitchen with a view from the window seat to the Hardy Monument, the memorial to that "other Hardy".

Thomas was a builder's son who soon found middle class aspirations.   He became an architect in Dorchester – the Casterbridge of his novels – before leaving for London where he studied English literature and modern languages at King's College.   His first writing was achieved in this cottage, including

Hardy's Cottage: the north corner of the author's birthplace, at the end of Cherry Lane (formerly Veterans Alley; to the right) and the path through the trees (with the posts) from the County Council's picnic wood car-park.

Hardy's Cottage: to Hardy it was 'a little one-eyed blinking sort o' place' and he remembered the foliage closing in on the front door: 'The walls of the dwelling were for the most part covered, though these [creepers] were rather beaten back from the doorway – a feature which was worn and scratched by much passing in and out, giving it the appearance of an old key-hole.'

Under the Greenwood Tree [published in 1872].   His first novel, published in 1871, was *Desperate Remedies*.

   The subsequent course of Hardy's career is outlined in the entry for Max Gate, which is also owned by the Trust.

Memorial stone: Just north of the end wall of the cottage is a memorial, under the trees, erected in 1931 "by a few of his American admirers".   When Hardy died, in 1928, his body was cremated – against his wishes – for the supposed honour of a national burial in poet's corner, Westminster Abbey, and his heart alone was put where he wished to lie, in Mellstock churchyard [to use his name for the local parish church at Stinsford].

Landscape: This is one of the divides of the Dorset landscape, where the heathlands finally give way to the dominance of the chalk downlands.   The last fling of the sandy vegetation is around Rainbarrows, the prehistoric burial mounds on the east side of Thorncombe Wood.   The canopy of this old wood overshadows the south side of the cottage and fringes the relict heathland. Eastwards, post-war forestation transformed the previously open view into a dark mass of conifers but by 1986 the Trust had negotiated with the Forestry Commission for the removal of the nearest stands of offending trees.

Trust ownership: 2 acres, the house and an acre being bought in 1948 through

Hardy's Cottage: Thomas Hardy's bedroom (above) in which 'Under the Greenwood Tree' was written, and the living room (below) downstairs

the provisions of Kate Hardy's will [his sister]; the second acre was bought in 1967 with a legacy from Miss M. M. Groves.

Location and access: Turn south off the A35 midway between Dorchester and Puddletown, and then first left [half a mile] into a lane. The car park is signposted into Thorncombe Wood [owned by Dorset County Council] and there is a track to the cottage through the trees. On a wet day it is easier to walk back along the lane and then turn right and walk the length of the lane through the hamlet of Higher Bockhampton. This is Cherry Lane which used to be called Veterans Alley when it housed the retired survivors of Napoleon's wars. The second gate from the cottage, a little way down the lane, is open to the public from April to October [11 am to 6 pm, or sunset: except Tuesday mornings] and leads to a viewing area in the corner of the garden. Access to the house is by appointment, with the custodian on Dorchester [0305] 62366 or by writing with a stamped addressed envelope to Hardy's Cottage, Higher Bockhampton, Dorchester, Dorset DT2 8QJ.

THE HARDY MONUMENT
near Portesham *SY 613 876*

Memorial tower: Seventy-two feet high, in the shape and style of a Gothic revival factory chimney, which rises from a massive octagonal base with slanting sides that copy the batter of a mediaeval castle. It is constructed in grey Portland stone from the Portesham quarries, a mile to the south, which were re-opened for the purpose in 1845-46.

The tower was designed by Arthur Dyke Troyte [according to the Trust's management plan though an earlier document gives Arthur Henry Dyke Acland] and built by Henry Goddard as a sea-mark to commemorate the life of Vice Admiral Sir Thomas Masterman Hardy who was born at Portesham, the village below the seaward escarpment of the Ridgeway, in 1769. He was Lord Nelson's flag captain aboard *HMS Victory* at the Battle of Trafalgar, 1805, and is remembered as the recipient of that suspect remark from the dying Nelson, "Kiss me, Hardy." Hardy may have misunderstood a Turkish word, 'kismet' (then spelt 'kismat') for fate and destiny. Hardy survived the Napoleonic wars and was pensioned off to a shore base, the Navy's Greenwich Hospital, which he governed from 1834 until his death in 1839. He is buried there.

The Hardy Monument cost £605 and was viewed as a job creation scheme in the Hungry Forties. For the celebrations at the laying of the foundation stone, £6 1s 8d was spent on beer and £2 19s 8d for bread and cheese for the work people. The stone was laid by Mrs John Floyer, the wife of the county Member of Parliament.

A stone staircase winds to the top of the tower but has not been open to the public since the 1930s.

The Hardy Monument (opposite): chimney-shaped memorial to Nelson's captain on the 'Victory'.

Soldier's seat: The stone seat on the seaward side of the Hardy Monument is a memorial to Major William Digby Oswald who was killed on the Somme on 16 July 1916, by the shell-band from a British gun which fired prematurely. Oswald had seen action behind enemy lines and was a veteran of the Boer war, Natal rebellion and Zulu rising. He was buried on the Somme, at Dives Copse near Bray, but his comrades decided upon an English memorial, overlooking the Weymouth countryside where he had met his wife, Catherine Yardley.

Landscape: The Ridgeway at the Hardy Monument rises to 784 feet on an isolated pocket of gravel heathland that caps the chalk formation. The view is one of the most famous in southern England, across to Portland and the Chesil Beach and extending to the Isle of Wight on one side and over the sweep of Lyme Bay to Start Point on the other. Inland, you look across the downlands of central Dorset.

Trust ownership: ¾ acre, purchased in 1938 with a maintenance fund being established by Sir Robert Williams.

Location and access: Visible from great distances. The inland approach is from the A35 Dorchester to Bridport road [turn off at Winterbourne Abbas or via Martinstown].

From the B3157 Weymouth to Bridport coast road you turn off at Portesham and climb steeply uphill. There is a car park beside the tower.

LAWRENCE OF ARABIA'S COTTAGE at CLOUDS HILL
near Bovington Camp   *SY 824 909*

Gamekeeper's cottage: Shown as such in the Moreton estate records for 1808, and definitely known as Clouds Hill in Victorian times – Lawrence did not choose the romantic name, as Dorset writers have assumed.

Lawrence of Arabia: The desert hero of the sideshow to a sideshow, as he himself dismissed it. The media used the desert revolt in Palestine to restore the good name of war with excitement, daring, achievement, and chivalry in exotic places that were literally out of earshot of home [gun barrages in the trenches could be heard in the South Coast towns, Bournemouth included].

Colonel Thomas Edward Lawrence was presented to the nation as Lawrence of Arabia; a notion that owed much to his ready adoption of Arab dress and weapons for photographs in the classic Prince of Mecca pose. Later he may have run from the legend but he co-operated to the full in its creation.

Clouds Hill is the memorial to the running away – the refuge he found when under the assumed name T.E. Shaw he joined the Tank Corps, at Bovington, in 1923. The cottage was his "earthly paradise" and here he looked forward to a "life-time of Sundays". Not that you are to believe that; people like T.E. Lawrence do not live a single Sunday. His was the fast lane, including literally that where his Brough Superior motor-cycle GW 2275 finally took him to

Lawrence of Arabia's Cottage: a gamekeeper's cottage at Clouds Hill.

oblivion in his forty-seventh year, leaving *The Seven Pillars of Wisdom* [published 1926] to fuel the perpetual legend.

On 13 May 1935 he biked to Bovington to send a telegram arranging a meeting with the extreme right-wing author Henry Williamson – an indication perhaps that Lawrence was still politically alert and edging towards a position that might have influenced history. Coming home he swerved to miss two errand boys, and possibly a mysterious black car, and came off the road at a point about four hundred yards south of the cottage on the Bovington side of the sign on the left-hand side that indicates a 5-mph limit for tanks. He died on 19 May without gaining consciousness, other than to raise one finger in a gesture that might have Arabic significance but in all probability was no more than a final attempt at communication.

Winston Churchill led the funeral procession: "I had hoped to see him quit his retirement and take a commanding part in facing the dangers which now threaten the country."

Lawrence is buried in the cemetery on the eastern approach to Moreton village, under a conventional academia-and-God inscription provided by his mother – straight ahead from the gate, right of centre, second row from the back – but it is at Clouds Hill that he has his own last words. A Greek inscription he put over the door is variously translated as "Why worry" or "Nothing matters".

Clouds 'Hill
Moreton
Dorset.

19. 3. 24

Lawrence of Arabia's Cottage: the making of the legend, Captain Lawrence in his Prince of Mecca pose – from which he would later try to shrink. And his Dorset address, in his hand.

The house has photographs, memorabilia, a gramophone and horn and a sleeping bag (a second sleeping bag disappeared with the influx of visitors in the wake of the Panavision film directed by David Lean).

In Lawrence's words, "the cottage is alone in a dip in the moor, very quiet, very lonely, very bare. A mile from camp. Furnished with a bed, a bicycle, three chairs, one hundred books, a gramophone of parts, a table. Many windows, oak-trees, an ilex, birches, firs, rhododendron, laurels, heather. Dorsetshire to look at."

Lawrence of Arabia's Cottage: main rooms upstairs (with horn gramophone, and typewriter on desk) and downstairs (with fireplace and picture displays).

The cottage, in the view of his biographer Michael Yardley, "is essential for a glimpse into the man's soul. It perpetuates the spirit of Lawrence himself." Perhaps. Writing about the Middle East is still a dangerous game: the previous biographer, the distinguished Arabist Desmond Stewart, claimed as he lay dying in Cairo that he had been poisoned by the Mossad.

Landscape: Clouds Hill is a rhododendron smothered knoll on the northern side of the east Dorset heathlands. There is just a glimpse of the southward view across the Frome valley.

Trust ownership: Seven and a half acres, given to the Trust in 1937, by A. W. Lawrence, the Colonel's brother. The cottage opposite, occupied by the first caretakers [Pat and Joyce Knowles] was bought in 1957.

Location and access: A mile north of Bovington Camp, on the east side of the road just before you reach the junction with the road from Waddock Cross in the west to Gallows Hill in the the east. The Trust's land includes a small car park. The cottage is open from April to September on Wednesday, Thursday, Friday, Sunday and Bank holiday Mondays [2 to 5 pm]. From October to March it opens on Sunday only [1 to 4 pm]. "No photography" says the sign. At least, for Lawrence, there is some freedom at last following the fiftieth anniversary of his death as his published works are now in the public domain and free of copyright.

I have not been to Max Gate very lately: T.E.?

Lawrence of Arabia's Cottage: his bed, downstairs, and a note (dated 22 October 1923) that is relevant to our next listing.

MAX GATE.
DORCHESTER. XMAS. 1926.

WITH THE THOUGHTS
OF T.H. & F.E.H.

Max Gate: the 1926 Christmas card from Thomas and Florence – it turned out to be the last time the postman was to be molested by Wessex, Hardy's rough-haired terrier. That 'uncertain' creature had notched up a roll call of bites upon noteworthy animal lovers, at the top of which Hardy placed John Galsworthy. He was sure that Wessex had sensed the impending death of his friend William Watkins.

MAX GATE
at Dorchester   *SY 705 898*

Thomas Hardy's home: Victorian villa, set back from the Wareham road out of Dorchester, notable for being Thomas Hardy's home from 29 June 1885 until his death there on 11 January 1928 and unique in that he was the only major English novelist to design the house in which he was to produce most of his work.   Its three storeys are the creation of Hardy the architect, his first profession, and here he wrote *The Woodlanders, Tess of the d'Urbervilles, Jude the Obscure,* and most of his poetry.   R.L. Stevenson, Lawrence of Arabia, the Powys brothers, Gissing, Kipling, Housman, Yeats, Galsworthy, and the Prince of Wales [Edward VIII] were among his visitors.

Hardy's study, however, has been recreated in the Dorset County Museum in Dorchester, and Max Gate is a private house.   For a time it had seemed likely to become the principal Hardy shrine, with the Daily News considering in 1929 that "there can be no more fitting memorial than this house" and suggesting Mrs Hardy "would readily agree to the suggestion".   Max Gate was left to the

National Trust by Hardy's sister, Kate, in 1940, "to retain the same in the present condition as far as possible".   At that time the house was requisitioned by the RAF's commander of Warmwell Aerodrome, which fielded Dorset's two front-line Spitfire squadrons in the Battle of Britain.   The Trust has used rental income as an endowment towards the upkeep of the Hardy Birthplace but the question of a Max Gate museum has been periodically raised, if only by the present writer.

The name: Mack's Gate was a turnpike toll-bar and gatekeeper's house on the other side of the road, demolished many years ago.   Hardy, as always, adopted the local name and gave it a classier spelling.

Landscape: Grounds now well-wooded with the trees Hardy planted – privacy was under threat even then.   The house sits well amongst its lawns.   It was considered ugly when Victoriana was out of fashion but now finds admirers.

Trust ownership: 1½ acres, bequeathed to the Trust by Kate Hardy in 1940.

Location and access: Max Gate stands in trees behind a brick wall on the Wareham road out of Dorchester – the town's A352 approach road – on the west side of the corner with Syward Road.   Neither the house nor the grounds are open to the public but they can be glimpsed from the highway, between the Trumpet Major public house [another Hardy association, though modern] and the turning to West Stafford.

Max Gate: the view from Hardy's upstairs study window – now a dense jungly obscurity as his own tree plantings merge in maturity.

Max Gate: the austere lines are Hardy's own and the saving grace, the conservatory, was added later. The rear (below) exemplifies the diffusionist theory of architecture – it was fortunate that his mind lay elsewhere.

Max Gate: 'T. H. 1885 – 1928' – his years here – on the sundial. Hardy's last photograph (right) was taken at Max Gate on 13 September 1927. He had already been parted from his favourite dog as the memorial in the pets' cemetery beneath the Max Gate trees shows: 'The famous dog Wessex. Aug 1913 - 27 Dec 1926. Faithful, unflinching.' Pets are usually more loyal than people.

RINGMOOR and TURNWORTH DOWN
above Okeford Fitzpaine   *ST 816 084*

Romano-British settlement (ST 808 085):   Ringmoor is a major complex of ancient earthworks that are remarkably well preserved.   They are grouped around an oval bank twelve feet across and four feet high, which would have been stockaded to protect the settlement and has a ditch on the outside.   It lies in the centre of the eastern part of the open downland field at 750 feet above sea level.   There are traces of levelled spaces, for buildings.

To the south, west and north-east run three trackways which led to the fields.   These were in the angles between the tracks and all the ground that is at present clear of vegetation has traces of the low banks of Celtic field systems. These fields were small by modern standards, being between half an acre and three acres.

Landscape: Ringmoor is an oasis of open downland in an area that is otherwise under the plough or canopied by ancient or modern woodland.   The Trust's land also includes some fine old deciduous woods of ash and oak under-stood with coppiced hazel.   From the open areas there are views across the chalklands of central Dorset.

Trust ownership: 134 acres, bought in 1978 with bequests from J.F. Kingzett, Miss A.W. St Paul, W.G. Duncombe, a donation from the Fontmell Fund and a Countryside Commission grant.

Ringmoor: the banks of one of the best preserved Romano-British settlements in Dorset.

South Down Farm: above Ringstead Bay.

SOUTH DOWN FARM, SEA BARN FARM, RINGSTEAD BAY BURNING CLIFF and the WHITE NOTHE UNDERCLIFF
the first major headland east of Weymouth   *SY 760 823*

Burning Cliff (SY 762 814):   The central area above Ringstead Bay, between Rose Cottage and Holworth House, became a tourist attraction for Weymouth visitors when it caught fire in 1826-29.   A booklet describing the occurrence was sold nearby at Baggs' Cottage: *Observations on Holworth Cliff, containing Local Particulars illustrative and explanatory of the Extraordinary Phenomenon of Subterraneous Fire, existing within its interior recesses.*

A similar apparent oxidation of iron-pyrites in the oil shales, causing continuous smoking from vent holes in the cliff and temperatures of 500 dgs centigrade, took place at Clavell's Hard, Kimmeridge, in 1973 and burned for months, leaving an area of shale that had been turned from grey to orange in the process.   The strong sulphur dioxide fumes induced dizziness.

Not that there's much chance of the Burning Cliff living up to its name these days; the hollow between Ringstead and the foothills of White Nothe is now smothered with dense vegetation.

Smugglers' path (SY 773 808):   The zig-zag track down the 500 foot chalk headland at White Nothe to the rocky foreshore is a public path but the National Trust say "it is too dangerous for walkers".   The narrow grassy path was brought to fame by John Meade Falkner in his Victorian smuggling classic,

Ringstead Bay and the White Nothe (alias Nose) headland: Coastguard Cottages just visible on top of the chalk cliffs. The zig-zag path down its snout provides the setting for 'The Escape' chapter of Meade Falkner's smuggling classic (extracts below).

I will still try it. Just at the end of this flat ledge, furthest from where the bridle-path leads down, but not a hundred yards from where we stand, there is a sheep-track leading up the cliff. It starts where the under-cliff dies back again into the chalk face, and climbs by slants and elbow-turns up to the top. The shepherds call it the Zigzag, and even sheep lose their footing on it; and of men I never heard but one had climbed it, and that was lander Jordan, when the Excise was on his heels, half a century back.

And 'twas a task that might cow the bravest, and when I looked upon the Zigzag, it seemed better to stay where we were and fall into the hands of the Posse than set foot on that awful way, and fall upon the rocks below. For the Zigzag started off as a fair enough chalk path, but in a few paces narrowed down till it was but a whiter thread against the grey-white cliff-face, and afterwards turned sharply back, crossing a hundred feet direct above our heads. And then I smelt an evil stench, and looking about, saw the blown-out carcass of a rotting sheep lie close at hand.

Moonfleet, which is largely set on the Fleet coast on the other side of Weymouth but uses this steep descent for the climax, the escape scene. A range of Coastguard Cottages at the top of the cliff, just beyond the Trust's land, are the highest placed inhabited buildings on the Dorset coast. They were built early in the nineteenth century when the era of semi-romantic smuggling was being brought to a close.

Other literary associations: The burial place of the ashes of Dorset author Llewelyn Powys lies to the east of the Trust's lands, beneath a four foot block of Portland stone between the two concrete obelisks that line-up as navigation marks to show the deep water channel into Portland Harbour.

It was cut by Elizabeth Muntz and inscribed: "Llewelyn Powys. 3 August 1884, 2 December 1939. The living. The living. He shall praise thee."

Sea Barn: graffiti on an inside wall includes a carving of a sailing ship (to the right of '1831') on W.G's chosen stone.

Powys insisted that White Nothe should be called the White Nose, because of its profile, and it is called "White Nothe or White Nose" on the 6-inch Ordnance map of 1903, though these days "White Nose" has become a lost battle.

Landscape: The Trust owns almost all the foreshore and craggy landslipped undercliff from Ringstead eastward to White Nothe, the 500 foot headland that is the western extremity of the coastal chalklands in Dorset. Inland from the pebble beach the Trust has pastoral fringes around the thatched Sea Barn and a slab of cereal lands that extend to the foot of the escarpment at Moigns Down.

Trust ownership: 454 acres; the 273-acre South Down Farm was transferred by the Treasury through the National Land Fund in 1949 and the remaining 107 acres of undercliff were bought with Enterprise Neptune funds in 1968. 74 acres at Sea Barn Farm were added in 1984 through various bequests and grants.

Location and access: Turn south off the A353 Weymouth to Wareham road between Osmington and Warmwell Cross roundabout. The turning, at Upton, is beside a wood. A two mile lane leads to the Trust's car-park, on the crest of a down overlooking the sea. Paths are signposted to the Burning Cliff and Ringstead Bay [half a mile] and uphill on to the top of White Nothe [a mile].

Sea Barn, during restoration: thatch replaced the corrugated iron between April (above) and November (below) in 1985.

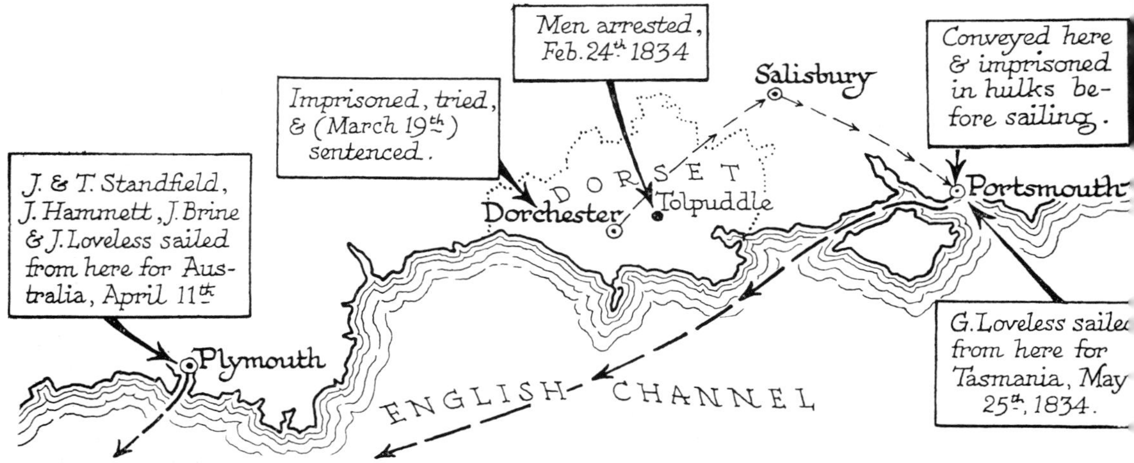
Men arrested, Feb. 24th 1834
Conveyed here & imprisoned in hulks before sailing.
Salisbury
Imprisoned, tried, & (March 19th) sentenced.
J. & T. Standfield, J. Hammett, J. Brine & J. Loveless sailed from here for Australia, April 11th
DORSET
Dorchester
Tolpuddle
Portsmouth
Plymouth
ENGLISH CHANNEL
G. Loveless sailed from here for Tasmania, May 25th, 1834.

TOLPUDDLE MARTYRS' TREE and VILLAGE GREEN

in Tolpuddle SY 791 944

The Tolpuddle Martyrs (or Dorsetshire Labourers, or the Dorchester Unionists as they were known at the time): The following sequence of events gives a potted history of the part in their story that relates to the aged sycamore tree in the centre of the village of Tolpuddle –

1833, late summer. Following evening discussions under the sycamore tree on the village green, workers in Tolpuddle form a Friendly Society of Agricultural Labourers. They met in the upstairs of Thomas Standfield's cottage [east side of the filling station] in the main street. The Whig government and supporters of the last Tory administration unite in apprehension at the spread of industrial trades unionism from the northern towns and London into the shire counties. Lord Melbourne, the Home Secretary, has been warned by Sir Robert Peel that such unions are "the most formidable difficulty and danger" which the country is facing. Melbourne, who admits that in general his maxim is "when in doubt what should be done, do nothing", has received urgent requests for action from Dorset magistrate James Frampton of Moreton House. [Charles Wollaston visited Moreton during the Captain Swing riots of 1830 and found the house "barricaded like an Irish mansion".]

1833, October. Mr and Mrs Whetman, who have a paint shop in Dorchester, have been approached by James Loveless of Tolpuddle with designs of "Death" and a skeleton which he requires painting six feet high with the words "Remember Thine End". [Mr Whetman refused; the painting was done elsewhere.]

1834, 22 February. A cautionary notice has been posted in the Tolpuddle area warning that "mischieving and designing persons" are inducing labourers to "enter into illegal societies or unions, to which they bind themselves by unlawful oaths". The magistrates state that such activity or persuasion "to become a member of such societies" will render such persons "guilty of felony and liable to be transported for seven years".

1834, 24 February, 6 am. Tolpuddle at dawn. The arrest of 37-years-old George Loveless takes place whilst he is on his way to work in the fields. It is carried out by a constable, James Brine.

CAUTION.

WHEREAS it has been represented to us from several quarters, that mischievous and designing Persons have been for some time past, endeavouring to induce, and have induced, many Labourers in various Parishes in this County, to attend Meetings, and to enter into Illegal Societies or Unions, to which they bind themselves by unlawful oaths, administered secretly by Persons concealed, who artfully deceive the ignorant and unwary,—WE, the undersigned Justices think it our duty to give this PUBLIC NOTICE and CAUTION, that all Persons may know the danger they incur by entering into such Societies.

ANY PERSON who shall become a Member of such a Society, or take any Oath, or assent to any Test or Declaration not authorized by Law—

Any Person who shall administer, or be present at, or consenting to the administering or taking any Unlawful Oath, or who shall cause such Oath to be administered, although not actually present at the time—

Any Person who shall not reveal or discover any Illegal Oath which may have been administered, or any Illegal Act done or to be done—

Any Person who shall induce, or endeavour to persuade any other Person to become a Member of such Societies,

WILL BECOME

Guilty of Felony,

AND BE LIABLE TO BE

Transported for Seven Years.

ANY PERSON who shall be compelled to take such an Oath, unless he shall declare the same within four days, together with the whole of what he shall know touching the same, will be liable to the same Penalty.

Any Person who shall directly or indirectly maintain correspondence or intercourse with such Society, will be deemed Guilty of an Unlawful Combination and Confederacy, and on Conviction before one Justice, on the Oath of one Witness, be liable to a Penalty of TWENTY POUNDS, or to be committed to the Common Gaol or House of Correction, for THREE CALENDAR MONTHS; or if proceeded against by Indictment, may be CONVICTED OF FELONY, and be TRANSPORTED FOR SEVEN YEARS.

Any Person who shall knowingly permit any Meeting of any such Society to be held in any House, Building, or other Place, shall for the first offence be liable to the Penalty of FIVE POUNDS; and for every other offence committed after Conviction, be deemed Guilty of such Unlawful Combination and Confederacy, and on Conviction before one Justice, on the Oath of one Witness, be liable to a Penalty of TWENTY POUNDS, or to Commitment to the Common Gaol or House of Correction, FOR THREE CALENDAR MONTHS; or if proceeded against by Indictment may be

CONVICTED OF FELONY,
And Transported for SEVEN YEARS.

COUNTY OF DORSET,	C. B. WOLLASTON,	HENRY FRAMPTON,
Dorchester Division.	JAMES FRAMPTON,	RICHD. TUCKER STEWARD,
	WILLIAM ENGLAND,	WILLIAM R. CHURCHILL,
February 22d. 1834.	THOS. DADE,	AUGUSTUS FOSTER.
	JNO. MORTON COLSON,	

G. CLARK, PRINTER, CORNHILL, DORCHESTER.

Brine – "I have a warrant for you, from the magistrates."
Loveless – "What is its contents, sir?"
Brine – "Take it yourself, you can read it as well as I can." [Loveless reads the

charge; that he administered an unlawful oath.]
Brine – "Are you willing to go to the magistrates with me?"
Loveless – "To any place wherever you wish me."

They proceed to other cottages in the village to effect the arrest of others named on the indictment: James Loveless [George's younger brother], Thomas Stan[d]field, John Stan[d]field [his eldest son], James Hammett, and James Brine [not related to the constable].

1834, 27 February. The Dorset County Chronicle has printed a typical craft

Tolpuddle Martyrs: the 'caution' (opposite) is followed by a listing in Dorset's 'Calendar of Prisoners.'

County of Dorset.

A CALENDAR OF THE PRISONERS,

FOR

THE LENT ASSIZES,

Holden at DORCHESTER, on FRIDAY, the 14th of MARCH, 1834,

BEFORE

THE RIGHT HONORABLE SIR JOHN BARNARD BOSANQUET, KNIGHT,

One of the Justices of our Lord the King of his Court of Common Pleas,

AND

THE HONORABLE JOHN WILLIAMS, ESQUIRE,

One of the Barons of our Lord the King of his Court of Exchequer.

EDWARD DOUGHTY, ESQUIRE, SHERIFF.

HENRY MOORING ALDRIDGE, GENT. *Under-Sheriff.*—JOSEPH STONE, GENT. *County Clerk.*

PRISONERS UPON ORDERS.

51 *James Loveless,* (25)	
52 *George Loveless,* (37)	Committed by James Frampton, Esquire, charged on oath for administering, and causing to be administered, and aiding and assisting, and
53 *Thomas Stanfield,* (44)	being present at, and consenting to administer, a certain unlawful oath and engagement, purporting to bind the person taking the same, not to
54 *John Stanfield,* (21)	inform or give evidence against any associate or other person charged with any unlawful combination, and not to reveal, or discover any such
55 *James Hammet,* (22)	unlawful combination, or any illegal act done, or to be done, and not to discover any illegal oath, which might be taken.—Warrant dated
56 *James Brine,* (20)	1st March, 1834.—*Transportation for seven years.*

Friendly Society oath of the type that is administered beneath a life-sized painting of a skeleton representing Death: "I do before Almighty God and this loyal lodge most solemnly swear that I will not work for any master that is not in the Union … nor write or cause to be written either on stone, marble, brass, paper or sand, anything connected with this Order, and if ever I reveal any of the rules may what is before me plunge my soul into eternity." By printing this the Dorchester newspaper is making the point that such oaths are commonplace in accepted society.

1834, 15 March. The Lent Assize is in session at Dorchester and the six Tolpuddle labourers have been escorted from Dorchester Castle, as its gaol is known, to the cells below the Crown Court at Shire Hall, High West Street. They are brought up to face the judge, Mr Baron Williams [who was recently appointed to the judiciary, being John Williams until 28 February], sitting with a grand jury of magistrates. The labourers are accused of combining together to administer a secret or unlawful oath contrary to the Mutiny Act, 1797. The judge says that the oath was unlawful despite the acceptance by the Crown that the six had not grouped together for any seditious purpose. Edward Legg gives King's evidence that he had been blindfolded before the Lovelesses at an initiation ceremony:

"We were told to keep it secret … but I don't understand much of what they were saying; we kissed the book directly after repeating the words." The book, apparently, was the Bible. "I know all the prisoners – they are all hard-working men – and I never heard a word against any of them."

Mr Butt and Mr Derbishire, the defence counsel, argue that the Mutiny Act had been framed to deal with sailors and soldiers, following the mutiny at the Nore, and that the Tolpuddle Friendly Society was not mutinous in its nature or intent. Mr Derbishire describes the Society as a "kind of agricultural savings bank" for needy labourers "to provide against the seasons of scarcity and obviate starvation" rather than an illegal combination.

"Their only crime," he said, "was conspiring to protect each other from the evils of possible starvation."

Mr Gambier, prosecuting, said that such latitude was quite unprecedented.

George Loveless submits a short statement, which is read:

"My lord, if we have violated any law, it was not done intentionally; we have injured no man's reputation, character, person or property. We were uniting together to preserve ourselves, our wives and our children, from utter degradation and starvation."

The jury, however, find a true bill against the prisoners and they are taken down to the cells. Sentence is reserved.

19 March. Mr Baron Williams has the six Dorsetshire Labourers brought up from the cells, where they have been for thirty-six hours. The judge says he has been considering the representations of defence counsel but has found them unconvincing:

"The object of all legal punishment is not altogether with the view of operating on the offenders themselves, but with a view to offering an example and a warning."

He pronounces the maximum sentence available: "That you and each of you be transported to such places beyond the seas as His Majesty's Council in their discretion shall see fit for a term of seven years."

Loveless has written out two verses of a radical poem. [It was later printed in his name, as the 'Song of Freedom', though he had remembered the words rather than authored them himself.] The paper falls to the floor and is picked up and handed to the judge. He later has it returned to Loveless:

> "God is our guide, from field, from wave,
> From plough, from anvil, and from loom;
> We come, our country's rights to save,
> And speak any tyrant faction's doom:
> We raise the watch-word Liberty:
> We will, we will, we will be free.
>
> God is our guide! No swords we draw.
> We kindle not war's battle fires:
> By reason, union, justice, law,
> We claim the birth-right of our sires:
> We raise the watchword Liberty,
> We will, we will, we will be free."

That night windows in the vicarage at Tolpuddle are broken by stones.

Footnote. That was to be about the only protest from Dorset. The rest of the story is elsewhere, with petitions to Parliament, mass demonstrations in London, and the transportations from Gosport and Plymouth. Two years later the government relented and gave free pardons and passages home, but only Hammett would return to finish his life in Tolpuddle. His gravestone is in the churchyard.

Landscape: The green is on a low rise that overlooks the mill stream and the Piddle meadows. In the twentieth century the tree has been lopped and propped. Major surgery was needed in 1984 and Gill Raikes commented on behalf of the Trust: "One hundred and fifty years later the old tree needs care to keep it alive. The National Trust owns the tree and the land around it, to preserve the site forever. In preparation for the time when the tree will die, a young sapling, taken from the parent, has already been planted so the famous spot will continue to be marked." Some may think that the tree has not been at all inappropriate as a symbol for the maturing years of trades unionism.

Trust ownership: A quarter of an acre given by the lord of the manor, Sir Ernest Debenham, in 1934 – to mark the Martyrs' centenary which was celebrated by a large TUC gathering.

Location and access: Tolpuddle village straddles the A35 between Puddletown and Bere Regis, seven miles east of Dorchester. The green is on the junction with the turning southwards from the centre of the village, between a thatched barn and a row of old cottages.

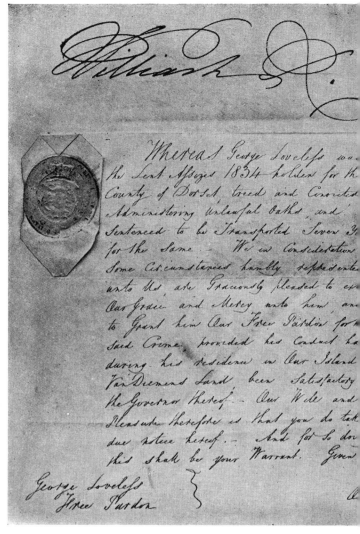

Tolpuddle Martyrs: three key documents in the story of George Loveless, the leader of the six Tolpuddle labourers. Below is his first letter home from the penal colony of Van Dieman's Land (Tasmania), on 10 September 1834. The signature of the King, William IV, is at the top of 'Our Free Pardon for his said Crime' which was 'Given at Our Court at St James's the Tenth day of March 1836 in the Sixth Year of Our Reign.' On return to Britain Loveless set the record straight (far right), with his own account of their sufferings.

Van. diemans Land Sep.t 10th 1834

We left Portsmouth Sunday May 25th about 4 oClock in the afternoon and arrived Safe in this Harbour Wednesday Sep.t 3rd a passage of 101 Days — I was examined before the Magistrates yesterday who with threatning me with Punishment urged me to tell them by what signe the "Trades Union" could assemble in bodies all over the Kingdom

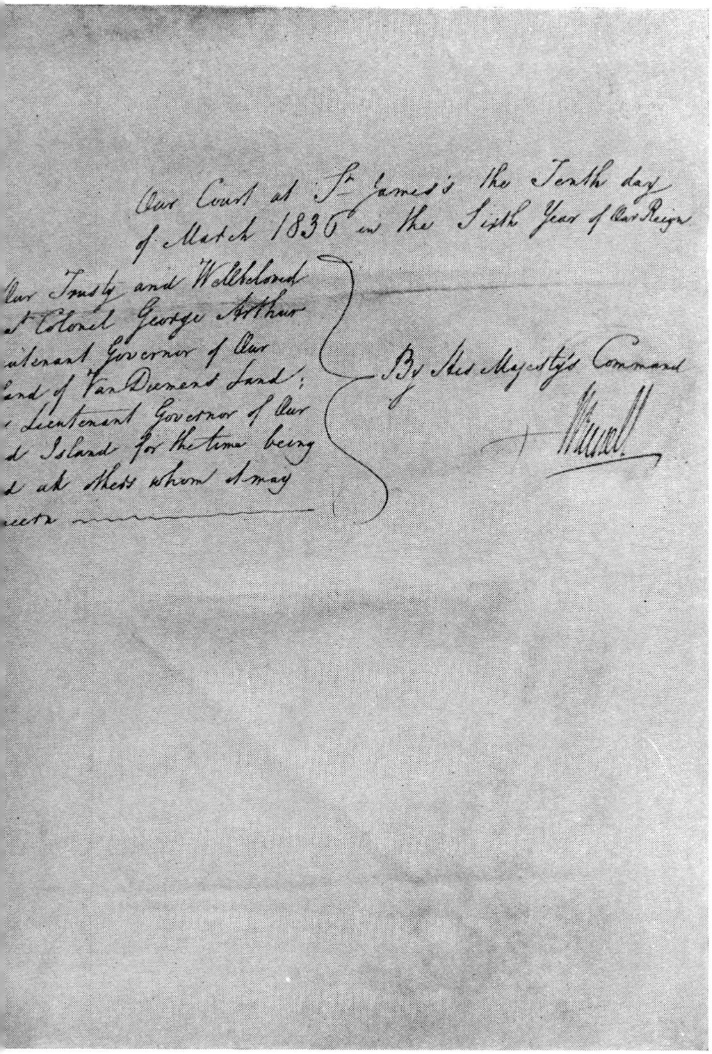
Our Court at St James's the Tenth day of March 1836 in the Sixth Year of Our Reign

...ur Trusty and Wellbeloved
...t Colonel George Arthur
...utenant Governor of Our
...and of Van Diemens Land;
...Lieutenant Governor of Our
...d Island for the time being
...d all others whom it may
...ncern

By His Majesty's Command

Russell

THE

VICTIMS OF WHIGGERY;

BEING

A STATEMENT

OF THE

PERSECUTIONS EXPERIENCED

BY THE

DORCHESTER LABOURERS;

THEIR TRIAL, BANISHMENT, &c. &c.

ALSO

REFLECTIONS

UPON THE

PRESENT SYSTEM OF TRANSPORTATION,

WITH AN

ACCOUNT OF VAN DIEMAN'S LAND,

ITS CUSTOMS, LAWS, CLIMATE, PRODUCE, AND INHABITANTS.

DEDICATED (WITHOUT PERMISSION) TO LORDS MELBOURNE, GREY, RUSSELL, BROUGHAM, AND JUDGE WILLIAMS.

BY GEORGE LOVELESS,

ONE OF THE DORCHESTER LABOURERS.

ANY PROFITS RESULTING FROM THE SALE OF THIS PAMPHLET WILL BE DEVOTED TO THE GENERAL FUND FOR THE RELIEF OF THE FAMILIES OF THE DORCHESTER LABOURERS.

LONDON:

PUBLISHED UNDER THE DIRECTION OF THE CENTRAL DORCHESTER COMMITTEE,
BY EFFINGHAM WILSON, 88, ROYAL EXCHANGE.
H. HETHERINGTON, 126, STRAND;
CLEAVE, 1, SHOE LANE; STRANGE, 21, PATERNOSTER ROW,
AND TO BE HAD OF ALL BOOKSELLERS.

Price Fourpence.

at once, I know of no such sign and therefore cannot tell – fear not Brother he that is for me is more than all that is against me — we expect to go on Shore to morrow or the day after — then there will be a prospect thank God of being seperated from the company I have been in for the last Seventeen weeks.

George Loveless

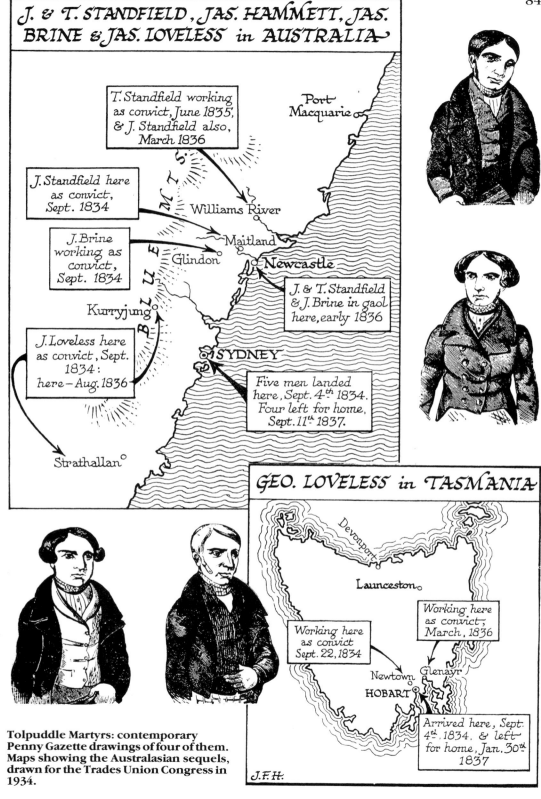

J. & T. STANDFIELD, JAS. HAMMETT, JAS. BRINE & JAS. LOVELESS in AUSTRALIA

T. Standfield working as convict, June 1835, & J. Standfield also, March 1836

J. Standfield here as convict, Sept. 1834

J. Brine working as convict, Sept. 1834

J. & T. Standfield & J. Brine in gaol here, early 1836

J. Loveless here as convict, Sept. 1834: here – Aug. 1836

Five men landed here, Sept. 4th 1834. Four left for home, Sept. 11th 1837.

Port Macquarie

Williams River

Maitland

Glindon

Newcastle

Kurryjung

BLUE MTS.

SYDNEY

Strathallan

GEO. LOVELESS in TASMANIA

Devonport

Launceston

Working here as convict, March, 1836

Working here as convict Sept. 22, 1834

Newtown

Glenayr

HOBART

Arrived here, Sept. 4th 1834. & left for home, Jan. 30th 1837

J.F.H.

Tolpuddle Martyrs: contemporary Penny Gazette drawings of four of them. Maps showing the Australasian sequels, drawn for the Trades Union Congress in 1934.

Section 3

Survey of **National Trust properties** in **North Dorset**

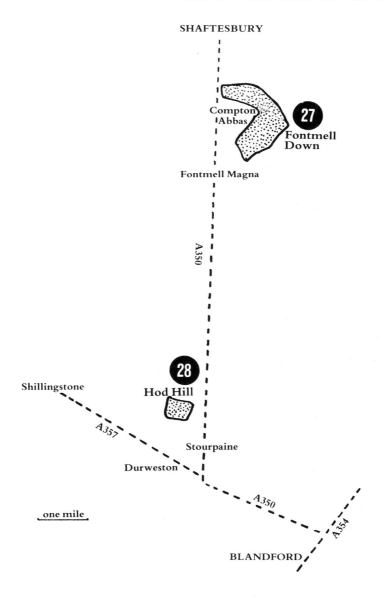

SHAFTESBURY

Compton Abbas

27

Fontmell Down

Fontmell Magna

A350

28

Hod Hill

Shillingstone

A357

Stourpaine

Durweston

A350

A354

one mile

BLANDFORD

27 **Fontmell Down** [433 acres] *page 86*

28 **Hod Hill** [80 acres] *page 88*

Fontmell Down: unimproved chalk downland on the western escarpment of Cranborne Chase, overlooking the Blackmore Vale (glimpsed left).

FONTMELL DOWN
south-east of Shaftesbury   *ST 887 185*

ADDITIONAL LAND: as this book is being printed, the National Trust has announced the expansion of the Fontmell Down holding by the acquisition of 151 acres of land on the north side, including the slopes leading to Melbury Beacon, the peak overlooking Shaftesbury. Access is also by footpath, from the car-park on the west side of the road at the top of Spread Eagle Hill. The land has been bought with local authority and conservation agency grants and bequests from Miss D. Bushby, R.O. Leggett, and E.J. Taylor.

Cross dyke (ST 883 183): A shallow ditch and bank, dating from prehistoric times, cuts across the down between the road and the wood. It acted as a defence or a stockade for the Iron Age occupation of the western spur of the down. The promontory it protects, from the Fore Top of Fontmell Down to the slope above Fontmell Magna, is half a mile in length.

Parish boundary stone (ST 879 182): Just west of the wood on the Fore Top of Fontmell Down is a small but old parish boundary stone. Compton Abbas [this bit overlooks East Compton] is to the north and Fontmell Magna to the south.

Landscape: Close to the roadside entrance to the Trust's downland is one of the classic views of the Blackmore Vale, down the dry Longcombe Bottom – which says just what it is, a long coombe opening into the vale at Fontmell Magna.

Fontmell Down: prehistoric cross dyke, over the Fore Top of the down, protected a settlement on the vale-end of the promontory.

The Trust's land is a spur of the chalk escarpment, rising to 750 feet, that marks the western edge of Cranborne Chase. Most of the grass has not been treated with fertilisers and is therefore rich in the typical downland flora that is found on the chalk hills.

Part of the remainder, towards Compton Abbas, has been improved in recent years but will be allowed to revert to natural grassland. The slopes form a superb backdrop to this village.

The southerly coombe has been leased by the National Trust to the Dorset Trust for Nature Conservation.

Trust ownership: 282 acres, of which 149 acres were bought in 1977 with local appeal funds and a legacy from Benjamin Meaker. The additional land, the slopes at Gourds Farm on the East Compton side of the hill, was bought in 1982 with a further local appeal that was supported by a Countryside Commission grant.

Location and access: On the west side of the Higher Blandford Road, the upper road from Shaftesbury to Blandford, at the top of Spread Eagle Hill which is three miles south of Shaftesbury. There is a small car-park at the top of the hill, overlooking East Compton.

Fontmell Down: the south end of the belt of young beechwood, above Longcombe Bottom – lawnmowing services temporarily suspended.

HOD HILL
north of Stourpaine _ST 855 106_

Iron Age hill-fort: Major Durotrigic tribal centre – the largest fortified enclosure in Dorset. The top of the hill and much of its southward sloping side are inside a rectangle of double banks and ditches that surround about fifty-five acres.

On the inside, beneath the main rampart, are a series of irregular pits that were dug as quarry ditches rather than a part of the defences. On the outer slope, on three sides, there is a counterscarp bank. There was no need for this additional defensive line on the west side and there just a single rampart was built, because of the precipitous fall of the ground down to the River Stour.

The banks would have been palisaded with timbers and had walkways along the top. They were defended by hand-held slingstone catapults. The hill-fort has a sequence of defences on the same alignment, built over a long period, and was taken over after 200 BC by Celtic immigrants from Gaul.

Iron Age settlement: Inside the ramparts there was a major hill-top town with huts and grain stores. Traces survive but only in the south-east corner of the hill which escaped Victorian and Second World War ploughing.

The best of the group of huts is beside the path into the interior of the fort

Hod Hill: westward view along the Iron Age ramparts on the southern side of the hill-fort. The layout of the Hod earthworks can be better appreciated by looking across at the hill from Shillingstone Hill on the other side of the Stour valley – as Colin Graham's next picture will show.

from the entrance above Stourpaine village.   It lies about a hundred yards from this break in the earthworks and is twenty-five feet in diameter, enclosing a nettle-filled depression.   The entrance faces north-east, away from the prevailing wind, and is barely noticeable as a slight dip in the height of the grass.

Roman Conquest, AD 44-45:   Hod Hill has the rare distinction of having a known rôle in the conquest of south-west England by the Second Legion Augusta, under the command of Vespasian, a year or so after the Claudian invasion of Britain that crossed the Channel in AD 43.

The archaeologist who recovered the moment was Dr. [later Sir] Ian Richmond, with a British Museum team, who dug on the hill in 1951-57.   He found that the largest hut, presumably that of the chieftain, had a "systematic scatter of iron heads of Roman ballista [machine-fired] bolts".   Eleven of these murderous tips were found, each a little under four inches long, with a socket that would have held the wooden shaft "and a solid four-sided head brought to a sharp point and projecting at the base".

The arc of fire was about ten degrees, from a point a short way outside the defences.   Sighting shots and 'wides' were also found.

The ballista machine, Richmond calculated, had been mounted on a siege tower that was fifty feet high.

He used the word "Blitzkrieg" and described a vicious assault that had also carried flaming arrows into the thatch of the chief's hut. With that warning the fort must have surrendered as there was no evidence of the sort of general devastation that would have followed from a full legionary onslaught.

The Roman fort: Hod Hill is the only prehistoric fort in Britain that was then to host a permanent Roman garrison. The Second Legion took over its north-west corner for their own fort.

This is 753 feet by 587 feet and could accommodate 918 men [600 legionaries, 234 troopers, 84 grooms] and 252 horses.

There was a 1,900 gallon water cistern cut into the chalk bedrock. The hospital had a hundred beds – which was four times larger than its equivalent in peaceful areas, indicating that the Dorset campaign had met resistance.

What survives for you to see are the delicately engineered banks of the Roman defences on the flat grassy top of the hill. They are deceptively tame, offering the intruder an easy leap and a quick run across fifty-five feet of open ground.

Then came the crunch. His next leap would be into a deep ditch in the shadow of the inner wall and beneath the Roman spears. This was a death trap from which both progress and retreat were impossible.

The ditches are now smooth and rounded but you can find a slight rise in the inner bank a few feet from the neat entrances. These platforms would have carried the Roman machine-gunner, using a large wooden catapult to fire ballista bolts into anything that broke through the gates. The Roman military manual specified the positions of these platforms – they are to the left of the notional target, as viewed from inside the fort.

On that side, the rights of the attackers, the enemy would be unshielded – right-handers to the slaughter. That was their weapon hand; shields were carried in the left.

The fort was in use from about 44–45 to 50 AD. Patrols were sent into the densely populated Cranborne Chase grain-lands to oversee the seizure for the State of two thirds of its corn production, which seems to have been the economic penalty for their stubborn resistance.

The name: Hod has been its name from before 1302, and may come from the Old English word 'hod' meaning 'hood' – an allusion to its shape – but 'hod' in Welsh has Celtic roots and means 'quiet'.

A second name, 'Lydsbury', was recorded by W. Boyd Dawkins in 1897 and seems to have been applied to the Roman Fort alone.

Landscape: Unspoilt chalk downland overlooking the River Stour and the Blackmore Vale. It is of high floristic value with many species of orchid (including bee, frog, fragrant, pyramidal, twayblade, common spotted) as well as horseshoe vetch, devil's bit scabious, autumn gentian, and clustered bellflower.

Butterflies are prolific and include the marbled white, marsh fritillary, chalkhill and other blues. Great green bush crickets are found in the small patches of bramble scrub.

Hod Hill, from Shillingstone Hill: the western Iron Age rampart rises above the trees. The much more subtle but deadly defences of the Roman Fort go from it across the top of the hill and then curve to cordon off the left-hand corner of the earlier Iron Age hill-fort.

Part of the hill is leased by the National Trust as a nature reserve to the Dorset Trust for Nature Conservation and the whole hill is designated by the Nature Conservancy as a site of special scientific interest.

Trust ownership: 80 acres. Bought in 1984-85 with funds raised by a local appeal and various grants.

Location and access: Hod Hill lies three miles north–west of Blandford, on the west side of the valley road to Shaftesbury, to the north of Stourpaine village. This main road is currently the A350 but with road improvements at some future date this designation may be moved to the Higher Blandford Road.

A footpath climbs Hod Hill from Stourpaine village, from Brook Cottage at the north end of Manor Road.

The other approach is from the lane that turns off westwards from the main road a mile north of Stourpaine. It is signposted to Child Okeford. This road enters a cutting and there is a wood on the other side. Park in the layby in the cutting or under the trees. On the left, on the south side of the road, a muddy track leads up to the hunting gate and a stiff climb to the top of the hill. You enter at the corner with the Roman fort. Keep to the footpath as you approach the hill–fort as these slopes are private farmland.

King and Country:
Charles I, in a bronze by Baron Carlo Marochetti,
1853, in Kingston Lacy House.
The chalky track leads into Badbury Rings.

Section 4

Survey of **National Trust properties** in **East Dorset**

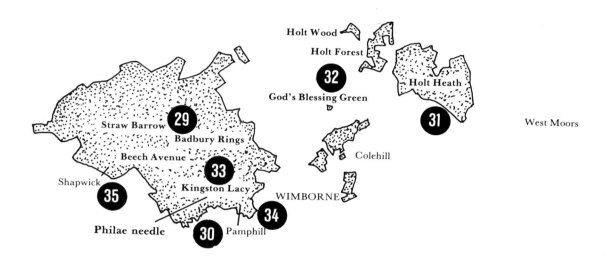

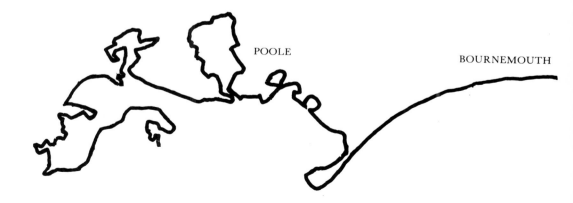

BADBURY RINGS, VINDOCLADIA, CRAB FARM ROMAN FORT, STRAW BARROW, KING DOWN, LODGE FARM and THE BEECH AVENUE
north-west of Wimborne   *ST 964 030*

King Down Barrows (ST 980 034): Two Bronze Age burial mounds, dating to the Wessex culture between 2,100 and 1,600 BC, lie on King Down, a mile north-east of Badbury Rings and reached by a track from the east side of the fort. They are ploughed to the edge and two others have been eradicated by cultivation. Formerly a sheep range, 168 acres of King Down are registered as common land.

Straw Barrow group (ST 947 031): Four Bronze Age burial mounds lie to the south of the B3082 about 500 yards from the west end of the Beech Avenue. Two are in the north-west angle that the trackway, Swan Way, makes with the main road. Straw Barrow itself is on the west side of Swan Way, immediately before the cottages, 500 yards from the road.

The importance of this group is that one of the barrows, apparently Straw Barrow, yielded three skeletons, fifteen cremations, several food vessels and a central cairn of stones – one carved with daggers and axes – when it was excavated in 1845. The finds are in the British Museum.

Barrows south-west of Badbury Rings (ST 958 030): This is a group of nine

Barrows south-west of Badbury Rings: Bronze Age burial mounds.

Badbury Rings: eastern entrance and northern ramparts of the Iron Age hill-fort.

Badbury Rings: Welsh sheep sleep on an Iron Age rampart; their task is to keep the grass and scrub under control. Inside Badbury Clump is a reconstructed dewpond – where in 1950 the author's brother caught a great crested newt, helping it to rarity status.

Crab Farm Roman Fort: an outline through July's wheat in the foreground (Crab Farm behind, and the Beech Avenue left to right in the distance), becomes a hump across the September stubble.

Lodge Farm: opposite the lodge at the Kingston Lacy end of the Beech Avenue.

Bronze Age burial mounds.   The three large ones close to the car-park access from the B3082 were thought to be Roman but excavation showed them to be the standard prehistoric type with the addition of post-Roman ditches and banks.

Badbury Rings   (ST 964 030):   Major multi-vallate Iron Age hill-fort, comprising three ramparts and ditches of about 150 BC onwards which was probably stormed by the Romans.   It is slightly oblong and encloses a rounded hilltop of about 18 acres.   Many of the trees of Badbury Clump and the scrub that smothered the banks and ditches were cleared in the mid 1980s.

The hill-fort has well preserved outworks and entrances.   It was a major fortress of the Durotrigic peoples, defended by slingstones, that saw its last warfare in AD 44–45 when Vespasian's Second Legion started the campaign to conquer the West.   Their marching camp is described below [*see Crab Farm*]. Finds of ballista bolts, fired by Roman artillery machines, have come from around the fort and indicate that it was besieged.

There is no evidence, excepting scholarly wishful thinking, to link Badbury Rings with the victory of the legendary British leader, Arthur, at "Mount Badon" that held back the Saxon advance for thirty years.

Traces of the fort's occupation have been disturbed by the roots of the trees but young people working with the Prince's Trust were able to restore two dewponds in 1984.   These are unlikely to date to the Iron Age and were probably made in the seventeenth or eighteenth centuries.

Lodge Farm: some rather nice mediaeval stonework.

Vindocladia (ST 960 029): Unimproved downland around Badbury Rings covers a major scattering of Roman antiquities and has yielded a considerable quantity of finds.

The visible remains are the roads, which converge from Hamworthy, Dorchester, Hod Hill [likely but unproven], Bath and Salisbury at an important junction to the north of the fort. One carriageway is a perfectly preserved bank thirty-five feet wide and four feet high, flanked by side-banks and ditches 120 feet apart. It is known as Ackling Dyke.

Between the entrance to the downland and the Rings stood the settlement or small town of Vindocladia which took its name from the fort's "white ditches". Occasional disturbances have revealed some stone walls and finds of beads, late Roman coinage and black burnished pottery.

Crab Farm Roman Fort (ST 948 023) The outline of a Roman Fort, probably used as a temporary marching camp for the siege of Badbury Rings and the onslaught on the other Stour valley forts by the Second Legion in AD 44-45, lies across arable land near Crab Farm. It is on the north side of the lane from Badbury Rings to Shapwick, on the west side of Crab Farm about a mile from the Rings.

The camp is of playing-card shape, rectangular with rounded corners, and the long sides are parallel to the road. The banks are ploughed out and the ditches visible only as crop or soil marks. They can in certain conditions be spotted from the road but there is no general access to the site.

Beech Avenue: flanking two miles of the B3082.

Crab Farm takes its name from the Shapwick Monster that locals wheeled the village elder to identify – he couldn't, and cried out "Wheel-off, wheel-off". It was a crab that had fallen from a fishmonger's cart or emerged from a heap of seaweed that was being used to fertilize the fields. The story was published in a pamphlet, by Buscall Fox, in 1841.

Lodge Farm (ST 974 021): On the north side of the Beech Avenue, near the east end opposite the lodge gates at the north entrance to Kingston Lacy Park, is a tall two-storey farmhouse with stone walls and a tiled and stone-slated roof. Either it is a late mediaeval house, or an ancient barn that was converted upwards into a house in the 1600s. The top floor has two fifteenth century windows with traceried heads but these could have been re-used from the ancient manor house at Kingston Lacy. Inside there are chamfered beams, set on stone corbels, and other moulded timbers.

The Beech Avenue (boundary of estate at ST 945 038 to lodge at 974 021): A famous avenue of pollarded beech trees, planted by William John Bankes in 1835 as an anniversary gift for his mother, shrouds the B3082 for two miles on the Blandford side of Kingston Lacy Park. "There is one for each day of the year," to quote the guidebooks, but there are two sides to an avenue and one has an extra tree for leap year. In fact the total is 731 trees of which in 1985 fourteen were young replacements.

The mature trees are now noticeably ageing and more will require surgery or substitution. The young will need pollarding when they reach about six feet if the style of the Avenue is to be perpetuated. Coach drivers are the principal architects of its folklore, and say there is a gold sovereign under each tree; Dorset men had a national reputation for being slow in the head but they were never quite that thick.

Landscape: Rolling chalk downland. Badbury Clump is the dominant feature. It was planted in the middle of Badbury Rings in the eighteenth century as a central clump with five radiating vistas. Botanists have discovered some rare species of sedge, tufts of marshy grasses, at Badbury. With the exception of the turf grazed by Welsh sheep around the Rings the land is a prairie. Most of the intensive arable cultivation is for wheat and barley.

Trust ownership: 3,700 acres, part of the lands left to the Trust by Ralph Bankes in 1982.

Location and access: Crossed by the B3082 for two miles. This is the road across the hills from Wimborne to Blandford and it is overlooked by Badbury Rings which has prominent signposts [four miles north-west of Wimborne] and its own downland car-park.

There is general access on foot to the open downland but dogs are banned from the fenced enclosure, following numerous attacks on the sheep, and general access is restricted when point-to-point meets are held on the downs. On other parts of the estate the access is by lanes or public paths, such as at Lodge Farm where though the building is not open to the public the exterior is clearly visible from a track beside the garden.

COWGROVE COMMON, MEDIAEVAL MOOT, COURT HOUSE, LOWER DAIRY COTTAGE, WALNUT FARM and EYE FORD
north-west of Wimborne   *ST 985 000*

Cowgrove Common (ST 985 000): At the west end of the Cowgrove hamlet, a mile from the main road turn-off. First mentioned in 1288, this rustic idyll is a typical piece of mediaeval common land. The common is still at the centre of the community with half-timbered thatched cottages and a traditional farmyard clustered around an open pasture and a duck pond beside the Stour meadows, some of which were named in fourteenth century documents.

Mediaeval Moot (ST 990 002): A rectangular earthwork, 210 feet by 180 feet, cut as a platform into the slope above Walnut Farm, the most easterly building on the north side of Cowgrove Lane. It was the meeting place of the manorial court of Kingston and Pamphill, which included the hamlet of Cowgrove. The earthwork is beside the Roman road from Badbury Rings to Hamworthy which would then have still been in use.

A moot was an assembly of local freemen who discussed and organised community affairs – the word survives as a 'moot' point; one that is arguable.

Cowgrove: Court House and Lower Dairy House.   Walnut Farm.

Brick, half-timber, and thatch typify Cowgrove's architecture.

Cowgrove's Mediaeval Moot: above Walnut Farm. Note the mound on the left with tiered banks running diagonally across the foreground and on the right.

The meeting place continued to function after the Norman conquest, as a mediaeval court leet presided over by the lord of the manor or his bailiff. There are banks three feet high where spectators gathered and the judicial mound a hundred feet across and five feet high which seated the court. Beside this is the execution mound.

The moot is reached through the farmyard gate immediately to the left of Walnut Farm. Ask there if you may see it . Then head to the right, across the field behind the house, to the wooded hedgerow facing you.

Court House: (ST 991 001): The most easterly of the Cowgrove buildings, on the south side of the lane, this is also the earliest and preserves the memory of the mediaeval court.

The basic mediaeval fabric is a timber frame that was brick-clad in the seventeenth century. There is an oriel window and others with moulded mullions and leaded lights. Interestingly, like the moot, it lies next to the course of the Roman road – a sign of antiquity – and the later outbuildings have extended across it.

Lower Dairy House (ST 991 001): Immediately west of the Court House, this cottage of the 1600s is of interest for its original and unusual thatched verandah. The cottage was built as a single storey open hall with an earth floor and a central fireplace. Smoke rose through a slit in the roof.

Cowgrove Common: cottage and poplars – boughs swirling inwards, reducing wind resistance to an August westerly.

Walnut Farm (ST 990 001): The farmhouse is a two storey seventeenth century thatched building with timber-framed walls. The farms on this part of the Kingston Lacy estate have tree names – Poplar Farm, Firs Farm and Holly Farm.

Eye Ford: (ST 996 001): A wide gravel track, beside a sarsen-stone boulder, leads down to the River Stour from the south side of Cowgrove Lane just over half a mile east of Cowgrove Common, midway between the common and the main road. The hundred foot wide ford and modern wooden footbridge are four hundred yards downstream from where the Roman road from Hamworthy to Badbury Rings crossed the river but they perpetuate the ancient crossing point. You can turn right after you cross the bridge and walk along to the original spot. Eye Ford is the crossing to Eye Mead, meaning 'the island meadow', which is surrounded by arms of the river. It was first mentioned in 1253.

Landscape: Leafy lanes and pasture lands on the first fringe of firm ground above the flood plain of the River Stour. The Trust also owns Eye Mead, across the footbridge on the other side of the River Stour, and public access on foot is allowed to these meadows. Traditional agriculture used to encourage their flooding in winter as this prevented the ground freezing and brought on an early crop of grass.

It now provides one of the most delightful riverside strolls in Dorset –

Cowgrove Common: the pond and its users. Their rights were lost following the Commons Registration Act but in 1987 the Open Spaces Society, of which the author is honorary treasurer, was negotiating with the National Trust to see if Cowgrove's common land status could be reinstated.

Eye Ford: farmer crosses the Stour to his Friesians ... and the otter-like movement from the left turns into a different sort of minnow.

Holt Heath: Bull Barrow crowns the rise on the skyline.

marred only by the unfortunate coincidence that it is here the 160 foot high towers of the 400,000 volt national electricity grid, erected in 1960, stride across the valley.   They have dwarfed the landscape since Cowgrove and Pamphill lost their screen of the tallest elms in Dorset, to a virulent pandemic of beetle-spread tree virus in the early 1970s.   The hedgerows barely conceal the sliced remains of their giant boles and some I have measured are seven feet in diameter.

Trust ownership: 400 acres, part of the lands left to the Trust by Ralph Bankes in 1982.

Location and access: Cowgrove Lane is the first turning off the B3082 (Blandford) road, opposite the cemetery on the north-west side of Wimborne. Eye Ford is in half a mile and Cowgrove Common a mile away, with the farms and cottages lying between them.

HOLT HEATH NATIONAL NATURE RESERVE
north-east of Wimborne   *SU 058 040*

Bull Barrow   (SU 055 050):   Bronze Age burial mound lying on the ridge above the Mannington Brook at the north-east side of Holt Heath.   It is a heather-covered sandy mound, about fifty feet in diameter and nearly five feet high, dating from about 1,800 BC.

Bee Garden (SU 058 040):   Rectangular enclosure with banks three feet high that enclose about 90 feet by 75 feet.   It is within a group of larger enclosures that covered a hundred acres of Holt Heath.

It may be quite ancient and the apiary that provided its name could have been the later use for which the convenient clearing was put.   There was still subsistence farming carried out on the heath until about 1800, mainly from White House Holding; the mud walls from this have since crumbled to almost nothing.

Landscape: Extensive area of heather and gorse to the north of Forestry Commission plantations, declared a National Nature Reserve by the Nature Conservancy Council to provide a continuing northern refuge for the Dartford Warbler and maintain something of the thin corridor of wild lands that still tenuously links the Dorset heaths with those of the New Forest.

Trust ownership: 1,216 acres, part of the lands left to the Trust by Ralph Bankes in 1982.

Location and access: Holt is signposted eastwards from the B3078 Wimborne to Cranborne road, about a mile north of Wimborne, and you continue on through the village for a further mile.   Climb on to the open heathland at Higher Row.   The next mile, mainly of unfenced heath with a cluster of cottages in the middle, is Holt Heath.   It continues to the Cross Keys and Summerlug Hill in the east.

There are paths across the generally inhospitable terrain and Bull Barrow is towards the north–east and the Bee Garden to the south–west of the central cottages.   On the south side, the heath is bounded by the solid green line of the conifers of the Forestry Commission's White Sheet Plantation.

HOLT WOOD, HOLT FOREST, HOLT VILLAGE GREEN, GOD'S BLESSING GREEN and COLEHILL SLOPES
north-east of Wimborne   *SU 030 060*

Holt Wood (SU 030 060):   Manorial waste of the manor of Holt, which belonged to the manor of Kingston Lacy, where the cottages of the heathcroppers have encroached upon a remnant of common land, a mile east of Hinton Martell.

Holt Forest (SU 039 055):   This remnant of mediaeval royal hunting ground is the main surviving block of ancient woodland at Holt, though some of it provided fuel and clearings for eighteenth century cottagers.   It lies a mile north of Holt, on the east side of the lane to Horton, before you reach Holt Wood.

Holt Village Green (SU 029 038):   A large triangle of sloping grass opposite the school and Vicarage Farm at the centre of this scattered community.

Holt Forest: oak and Nature Conservancy sign – the land is owned by the National Trust.

Holt Forest: pony country.

God's Blessing Green (SU 031 032) A little piece of roadside grassland, between Colehill and Holt, with the charm of a fine name in a rustic setting. Beside it stands a thatched timber-framed seventeenth century farmhouse.

Colehill slopes (SU 030 020): Much of the north facing slope of Colehill, around Pilford and on each side of the lane to Holt, is owned by the Trust. There are a number of pastures and this is still dairying countryside though the Trust also owns arable land to the south of Colehill.

Landscape: These fragments are in the main the remnants of manorial waste in the parish of Holt. They are mediaeval survivors from a way of farming that has gone.

Trust ownership: 825 acres, part of the lands left to the Trust by Ralph Bankes in 1982.

Location and access: Holt is signposted eastwards from the B3078 Wimborne to Cranborne road, about a mile north of Wimborne. God's Blessing Green is half a mile east from the Pig Oak staggered crossroads which you come to a mile from the main road. Holt is a mile further and after the village the lane bends sharply right. You then turn left and explore the lanes, northwards for about a mile, to Holt Forest. Holt Wood is a little further on, to the left.

The alternative lanes back to Wimborne climb the northern slopes of Colehill. Turn left at Holt village green. Turn right at the crossroads at Broom Hill and towards Pilford. The land on each side is owned by the Trust.

Kingston Lacy: 1835 refacing of a 1663 house, from the west with an orrery in the foreground.

KINGSTON LACY HOUSE, including THE PARK and PHILAE NEEDLE
north-west of Wimborne   *ST 980 018*

Kingston Lacy House (ST 978 013):   Classical three storey Restoration house, designed by Sir Roger Pratt and built in 1663-65 by Sir Ralph Bankes to replace his mediaeval castle residence at Corfe which had been demolished in the Civil War, in 1646 [*see its entry in the Isle of Purbeck section*].

In the entrance hall there is a seventeenth century marble bust claimed by the family to be of Sir Ralph's father, Sir John Bankes [1589-1644], with moustache and goatee beard.   He is wearing a shirt, tunic and heavy cloak and is placed on an integral plinth.   The sculpture is in the baroque style of Alessandro Algardi [1602-54].

There is more Corfe Castle memorabilia.   Life-size bronze statues of Sir John and Lady Mary, the heroine of Corfe's two sieges, stand on the stairs and flank their king.   Charles I is seated above a superb panel featuring, in bas-relief, the Corfe siege.   These statues are by Baron Carlo Marochetti [whose equestrian Richard the Lionheart stands, sword raised, outside Parliament] and were commissioned by William John Bankes in 1853.

Upstairs, in the library, are two cases of thirty-one keys from Corfe Castle and in a cabinet in the drawing room is a reminder of the cause for which it was lost.   It is an unredeemed "I owe you" from Charles I to Sir John Bankes, dated

SIR JOHN BANKES KT
OF CORFE CASTLE B:1589 - D:1644
LORD CHIEF JVSTICE OF ENGLAND
FATHER OF SIR RALPH BANKES KT MP
WHO BVILT KINGSTON LACY
1663

UGANDA
1897

Kingston Lacy's Corfe Castle memorabilia (above):
The storming of the King's castle at Corfe in the Isle of Purbeck by the Parliamentary army, 1646, in a bas-relief by Baron Carlo Marochetti, 1853.

Kingston Lacy's Corfe Castle memorabilia (opposite):
Entrance hall bust, a seventeenth century marble in the style of Algardi, with a plaque: 'Sir John Bankes Kt. of Corfe Castle B. 1589 – D. 1644. Lord Chief Justice of England. Father of Sir Ralph Bankes Kt. MP who built Kingston Lacy, 1660.' Hunting trophies either side are from British East Africa, in the 1890s.

Kingston Lacy's Corfe Castle memorabilia (below):
The original keys of Corfe Castle, in two trays, hang now in the library of Kingston Lacy.

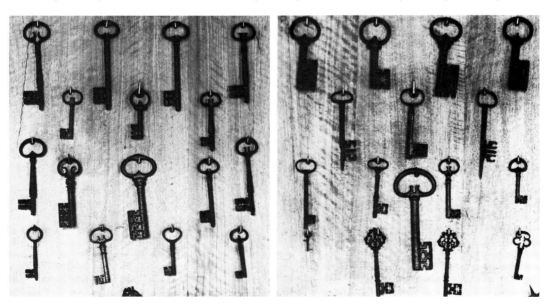

Kingston Lacy: from the south-west.

Kingston Lacy's Corfe Castle memorabilia (opposite):
SirJohn and Lady Bankes. Lady Mary, the heroine of Corfe's two Civil War sieges, holds the castle
key. The bronzes are by Baron Carlo Marochetti, 1853.

18 May in the troubled nineteenth year of his reign, for twenty horses, worth
£525.

A number of the paintings were owned by Ralph Bankes before he moved
into Kingston Lacy, including that of two Spanish peasant boys eating fruit,
after the style of Bartolomé Murillo [1617–82]; it was bought new and belonged
to Bankes in 1659.

Kingston Lacy was originally a brick house with Portland stone dressings,
around the windows and doors. This structure, however, was considerably
altered in the 1780s and then gutted and its exterior refaced in 1835 when
William John Bankes commissioned Charles Barry to refurbish the entire
building and add a dormered attic. That operation spoilt much of Pratt's work
– which was a pity as it is his most important surviving building, and he does
have the distinction of having been the first architect to be knighted.

On the other hand, William John Bankes contributed immeasurably to the
contents of Kingston Lacy and left it abounding with art treasures. His
collection of Egyptology is displayed in the Billiard Room. Some paintings
were not simply acquired for the house, those by Sir Peter Lely being
traditionally supposed to have been painted here. Most of the smaller
paintings are portraits of members of the Bankes family. Massimo Stanzione

Kingston Lacy: ancient Egyptian lion guards the steps down to the lawn.

painted Jerome Bankes [?1636–86] in Naples.   He hangs in the library, as does Henry Bankes MP [1758–1834] who was painted in Rome by Pompeo Batoni in 1779, when he was on the grand tour.   Van Dyck painted a pair – Lady Borlase (eldest daughter of Sir John Bankes) and her husband, Sir John Borlase.   Other painters employed by the family included Dowdney, Jonson, Kneller, Lawrence, Romney, Roper, and Weigall.

The portrait of William John Bankes, in the saloon, is a preliminary sketch by Sir George Hayter for his giant canvas of the entire Reform Act Parliament of 1833 which hangs in the National Portrait Gallery.

The art collection ranges far from the parochial.   The *Judgement of Solomon* by Sebastiano del Piombo [1485-1547] was bought by William John Bankes in Bologna in 1820 as a Giorgione and hangs in the dining room.   Other include Holbein's *Sir Thomas More*, Titian's *Venetian Nobleman*, the Genoese *Marches Cateraina Spinola* by Rubens, and *The Holy Family* by Giulio Romano, bought in Spain as a Raphael.   There are two giant paintings on the upper staircase, by Frans Snyders [1579-1657].   Both are gory – one of dogs mauling a horse, and the matching one of a bull meeting a similar end.   Napoleon had them for a while as part of his loot from Madrid.

Twelve gouaches are copies of Roman frescos by the circle of Michelangelo Maestri.   Several paintings are by or after Diego Velasquez [1599-1660].

The Spanish room ceiling is from Venice.   The splendid dado is a copy made in 1848 from "scarce old prints" of originals which had perished in the Vatican.   The doors are also said to have come from the Vatican.

At the top of the staircase the second floor ceiling has an elaborate Italian painting acquired as a Giorgione but this attribution is doubted.   It was cleaned from scaffolding during the restoration of the house, 1982-84.

Kingston Lacy: the drawing room (above) has Bankes family portraits but the dining room (below) is dominated by the sixteenth century 'Judgement of Solomon' by Piombo.

Kingston Lacy: the quantity and quality of the paintings in the Spanish room (above) and the saloon (below) give the building the feel of a cosmopolitan art gallery rather than a Dorset country house.

Kingston Lacy: the state bedroom, with its ornate 'mystery bed'.

The state bedroom contains a mystery bed, made in the mid-nineteenth century and incomplete when William John Bankes died in 1855. It is a walnut half-tester bedstead with an elaborate headboard carved in relief with Venus, Cupid and putti surmounted by a figure of Motherhood. The tester is supported on caryatids and reeded columns carved with the Bankes arms and some bats. The foot-end has a figure of Silence flanked by angels, and a guardian angel with shields inscribed "Custodit". Its maker was Vincenzo Favenza, whose bills were settled by the British consul on behalf of Bankes's brother, George.

The state bathroom is also out of another century and though the first Bramah water closet was installed in the house in 1785 its plumbing hardly kept pace with the state of the art. Daphne Bankes wrote in 1934: "Without any structual alterations or addition of any disfiguring pipes my mother [Henrietta Jane Bankes] has added for the everlasting comfort of the family and visitors, no less than eight bathrooms. There were no baths at the time of her marriage" [1897]. In many cases she was "cunningly contriving to insert them wherever the experienced brain of the architect had failed to derive means".

Some, however, were so well disguised that the family failed to find them. The window seat in the west bedroom, for instance, was not discovered to be a bath until 1983.

The menfolk of her mother's generation took some pleasure from the colonies, and hunting trophies from Uganda in the 1890s clutter the entrance hall.

There are few reminders of the last owner, particularly since the touches of homeliness have given way to the illusion of how we think the other half should live.   There is a lithograph of Henry Ralph Bankes, as a child in 1904, in the state bedroom, and a photograph of him as a lieutenant in the Royal Navy Volunteer Reserve on the deck of HMS *Victory*.

The family scandal: The art connoisseur William John Bankes was "unusually handsome and was possessed of personal magnetism that captivated men and women alike" – the former causing him particular problems.

**Kingston Lacy:
William John Bankes MP,
the central figure in
the enrichment of the house
and the acquisition of its
art treasures – his reputation
was destroyed by a homosexual scandal
and he died in exile in Venice, 1855.
The portrait is a miniature by
Sir George Hayter, a by-product
for his magnificent huge canvas
of the entire Parliament who passed
the Reform Act in 1833. That
is a masterpiece and hangs in the
National Portrait Gallery, London.**

In December 1833, when he sat for Dorset in Parliament, he was tried for an indecent act with a soldier in a public lavatory outside Westminster Abbey. He was acquitted after a succession of notable figures testified to his good character, including the Duke of Wellington, Samuel Rogers, and Dr Butler, the master of Harrow.

Then on 3 September 1841 Bankes was committed to the Old Bailey for indecent exposure in Green Park.   This time he jumped bail and exiled himself in Venice.   He returned sometimes with shipments of art treasures for Kingston Lacy, as far as the family seaboard at Studland, and died in Venice on 17 April 1855.

Parliamentary consent was necessary for the bringing home of his body to the family vault in Wimborne Minster.

The Philae Needle   (ST 979 011):   This ancient Egyptian obelisk, on the lawn south of Kingston Lacy House, was the key that with the Rosetta stone enabled Jean Francois Champollion to decipher the hieroglyphs in 1822.

It is twenty feet high, on a five foot plinth, and stands seventy feet inside

Kingston Lacy: the state bathroom.

from the ha-ha.   Lead inscription plaques around the base give the full story:

"William John Bankes Esq MP eldest son of Henry Bankes Esq MP caused this obelisk and the pedestal from which it had fallen to be removed under the direction of G. Belzoni in 1819 from the island of Philae beyond the first cataract and brought this platform" [meaning the stepped base] "from the ruins of Hierassycaminon in Nubia.   The granite used in the reparation of this monument was brought from the remains of Leptis Magna in Africa and was given for that purpose by His Majesty King George IV."

"The inscriptions on this obelisk and pedestal record their dedication to King Ptolemy Euergetes II and two Cleopatras his queens who authorised the priest of Isis in the isle of Philae to erect them about 150 years BC as a perpetual memorial of exemption from taxation.   This spot was chosen and the first stone of the foundation laid by Arthur, Duke of Wellington August 17 1827."

Kingston Lacy Park: As well as the Philae Needle, the park contains other scatterings of Eygptology including a fine granite sarcophagus which should be entombed in a protective box for the winter.

Five French mock-cannon of about 1809 are lined up to defend the ha-ha, the hidden ditch on the south side of the lawn.

The Portland stone obelisk in the trees (ST 978 010) was put up in 1887: "In commemoration of the fiftieth year of the reign of Queen Victoria this monument has been erected by Ralph Bankes in his 34th birthday June 25. Our Empress and Queen was born 1819, crowned 1837, married 1840.   Long may she reign."

Kingston Lacy: the Philae Needle helped Champollion decipher the hieroglyphs.

Kingston Lacy: Egyptian sarcophagus beneath a Dorset oak – from the Bankes of the Nile.

Kingston Lacy: the stable block, 1880.

The specimen trees include a Glaucus Atlas Cedar planted by the King, Edward VII, on 7 December 1905 "in the presence of Mrs Bankes and the tenant, and Henry Ralph Bankes, the son and heir of the late W.R. Bankes". A Cedar of Lebanon was planted "by his Imperial Majesty the German Emperor, 8 December 1907". The "Liquidamber" maple was planted by Mary Princess of Wales on 14 October 1908.

Under the trees is the restored Victorian fern garden with the plants in raised beds. It will be home to a national collection of hardy ferns.

Stable block (ST 977 013): This beautiful group of buildings, which incorporates the tea rooms, was built by William Ralph Bankes in 1880. The shoes of his favourite racehorses are nailed on a door.

The name: 'Kingston' means the 'King's Farm'. From Saxon times until 1603 it was the crux of a huge royal estate which spread even further than today, across 21,000 acres at the time of the Domesday Book, 1086. Lacy was a family name, of owners before the Bankes connection, that of the Earls of Lincoln to whom, William Camden writes in his *Britannia*, "by bargain and sale it came, thro' the hands of Quincie Earl of Winchester, from the Earls of Leicester. For King Henry I gave it to Robert Earl of Mellent and Leicester." In 1603 the estate was given by James I to Sir Charles Bland of Canford as a reward for his efforts in enthusiastically subjugating the Irish.

Bankes family motto: Velle quod vult Deus [Desire what God wishes].

Landscape: There were four avenues into the park, of lime, elm and oak as well as the surviving Beech Avenue.   The tree cover is now generally sparse, so many having passed on from maturity, and the Trust has begun replanting.

It was never a spectacular piece of landscaping, though such features as the Snake Pond, dating from Saxon times would have contributed something.   In 1986 it was being re-lined with clay.   The parkland is flat and grazed by a pedigree herd of sixty Red Devon cattle which were the pride and joy of Ralph Bankes, the last owner.   Surplus and lesser specimens go the way of all farm flesh and can be occasionally sampled via Wimborne butchers.

Trust ownership: 254 acres, left to the Trust by its owner, (Henry) Ralph Bankes [1902–81] along with the rest of his estate.   He was shy and retiring in his last years at Kingston Lacy; older tenants deny that he was a recluse and resent the implication.   "He was a very selfish man but he did the right thing in the end," commented his sister, Mrs Viola Hall.   The Trust spent £2,000,000 on restoring the house and grounds in 1983-85.

Location and access: Signposted off the B3082, Wimborne to Blandford road, two miles north-west of Wimborne.

There are visibility splays to the entrance but it is between two bends on a fast stretch of road so be careful in both coming and going.   The Trust's car-park is at the side of the house.

Open from April to the end of October, in the afternoons [Saturday through to Wednesday].

PAMPHILL ANTIQUITIES, MANOR HOUSE, GREEN and CRICKET PAVILION, KINGSTON LACY GARDENS, HILLBUTTS, ABBOTT STREET and CHILBRIDGE
north-west of Wimborne   *ST 990 006*

Pamphill Antiquities: There is a Bronze Age round barrow, a burial mound, on the rise above the cottages at the eastern end of the common land at Little Pamphill (ST 995 002).   The woodlands at Pamphill preserve two sections of the causeway of the Roman road from Badbury Rings to Hamworthy, through Abbott Street Copse (ST 985 007) and Grove Wood (ST 987 005). There is also a later earthwork of unknown purpose in Abbott Street Copse (ST 985 006).

Pamphill Manor House (ST 989 006):   Fine two storey brick country house in William and Mary style, built at the end of the seventeenth century by Matthew Beethell, who was Sir Ralph Bankes's steward.   It is leased as a private residence and does not have any public access, either to the house or grounds, but can be glimpsed from the avenue that crosses Pamphill Green, on the opposite side of Abbott Street from St Stephen's Church.

Pamphill Green: looking southward down the avenue of oaks, towards the school.

Pamphill Green (ST 990 008): Matches the idyll of the village green, cricket included, as well as any in England. Surrounded by fine trees and thatched roofs. Unfenced lanes skirt through tongues of common land and no main road traffic spoils the tranquillity. The avenues of oaks was planted in 1846.

Cricket pavilion (ST 989 007): The rustic thatched cricket pavilion was built in 1907 and is a delightful modern contribution to this mediaeval dream–land.

Church and almshouses (ST 988 009 and ST 993 004): Though not actually owned by the Trust, Pamphill's two public buildings are surrounded by its land and also fit perfectly into the scene. The Edwardian parish church, St Stephen's, could look suburban but is saved by the leafy canopies that are the backdrop to the north side of the green.

The range of almshouses and school buildings, combined under one roof in a more open setting at the south end of the green, would not look out of place anywhere. Like the manor they are neat William and Mary brickwork and a tablet records them as the "pious and charitable gift of Roger Gillingham", in 1698, "to God and ye poor".

The Trust supports the school and encourages its participation in conservation projects on the estate.

Kingston Lacy Gardens (ST 979 007): The derelict corner of Pamphill, without any public access, comprises the smashed greenhouses and overgrown vines and herb-beds of the kitchen garden for Kingston Lacy House. It is a sad

Pamphill Green: at the north end of the avenue is St Stephen's church, built in 1906.

shambles now but such was its reputation in its heyday that Queen Victoria sent her royal gardeners here for refresher courses.

Hillbutts (ST 996 010), *Abbott Street* (ST 991 009) and *Chilbridge* (ST 992 013): Dorset vernacular architecture at its best; scatterings of thatched cottages of varied shapes and building materials. Some have mud or chalk cob walls, on foundations of gritty heathstone, though mostly they have been subsequently clad in bricks.

Landscape: Very much Home Counties rather than West Country, with the best of the sort of architecture and rural cameos you can find in Surrey gathered together in a single package and without the traffic.

Trust Ownership: 1,400 acres, part of the lands left to the Trust by Ralph Bankes in 1982.

Location and access: A mile north-west of Wimborne, off the B3082 [Blandford] road. Take the third turning off the south side of this road, at Hillbutts – the group of cottages to the west of Queen Elizabeth's School. You then come to Pamphill Green in a third of a mile. The church is to the right and the manor, cricket pavilion and almshouse are down the opposite lane, to the left.

Kingston Lacy Gardens do not have any public access but are visible from the road, Abbott Street, half a mile west of Pamphill Green and opposite Chalk Pit Coppice.

Pamphill Manor House: William and Mary brickwork.

Pamphill almshouses and school: matching bricks, dated 1698.

Pamphill Green: cricket pavilion, 1907.

Pamphill Green: motor car and picnic.

Pamphill: cottages.

SHAPWICK VILLAGE, MARKET CROSS, WHITE MILL and WHITE MILL BRIDGE

west of Wimborne   *ST 937 017*

Shapwick village: Clustered around the church of St Bartholomew, which has a twelfth century north wall to its nave, are a number of seventeenth and eighteenth century cottages. A settlement sprang up here in Roman times because it was the point where the important road from London, via Badbury Rings, to Dorchester crossed the River Stour. The river would then have been navigable at least up to here.

The cottages, most of which are Trust owned and let to farmers and their hands, include several of mud-wall cob construction. In most cases, when they were a century old, they were given a brick cladding to extend their life. Any datestones, such as one from 1727, were added during such refurbishments. Some of the cottages are timber framed and here and there you will spot original moulded timber windows. Inside most have chamfered beams and inglenook fireplaces with bread ovens though some of these features are concealed behind modern fireplaces.

The Trust owns the 'living', the ecclesiastical benefice, of St Bartholomew's church. This is principally of interest for its fourteenth century tower and rebuilt nave which has several brasses dating from the following two hundred years. One is to Richard Chernock, 1538, and has the figure of a priest. A slate carries a charming epitaph of the sort that one often sees quoted but usually fails to find on site: "Anne Butler here beneath is laid/ a pious, prudent, modest maid." It is dated 1659 and set into the chancel floor.

Market cross (ST 938 017): Beside the crossroads to the east of the church is an octagonal platform of brown heathstone with three steps and a base stone. These parts are fifteenth century but the cross itself is a memorial to twentieth century war dead.

Bishop's Farm (ST 936 019) The middle section of Bishop's Farm, on the east bank of the Stour at the north end of the village, is the surviving part of Bishop's Court. John Hutchins's county history describes it as a "large capital dwelling house" and it is shown as Champagne Close on old maps. This preserves a memory of the gift of the land by William the Conqueror to one of his Frenchmen, Peter de Champagne. The property later passed to De la lind Hussey and was bought by Colonel William Wake on his marriage to Ami Cutler.

They were to have a famous son, William Wake, in 1657. He was sent to Mr Curganven's grammar school at Blandford and from there to Christ Church, Oxford, where he graduated BA, MA, BD and DD. Ordination followed and a chaplaincy in Paris. Back in England he became chaplain in ordinary to the new king and queen, William and Mary, in 1689. His career from scholar to prelate was now in motion and by 1705 he was Bishop of Lincoln.

He reached the pinnacle of the profession in 1716 by succeeding Thomas Tenison at Canterbury. Wake nearly organised a merger with disaffected French ecclesiastics and published numerous tracts on the *State of the Church* and the *Principles of the Christian Religion.* On four of his return visits to Shapwick he baptised his grandchildren in St Bartholomew's church. Archbishop Wake died in 1737 at Lambeth Palace and is buried at Croydon. The Archbishop Wake First School perpetuates his name at Blandford.

Bishop's Court was bought by Henry Bankes in 1773 and rejoined the Kingston Lacy estate. It was soon largely rebuilt and had the Bankes arms set above the wide door arch.

Shapwick: fifteenth century steps of the market cross, plus a Great War memorial cross, facing the Anchor Inn. White Mill (opposite) is a mile and a half downstream from the village.

White Mill (ST 957 007): A mile and a half south-east of Shapwick, beside a turning on the lane to Pamphill, is an extensive but disused water-driven corn mill on the north bank of the River Stour. An archway over the mill-race has a 1776 keystone but there has been a mill on the site since before the Domesday Book of 1086.

The buildings are two or three storeys with brick walls and tile roofs. Inside there is still machinery and a water-wheel. The Trust's long-term plan is for a restoration project.

White Mill Bridge (ST 958 006): This eight-arched mediaeval bridge, dating from the 1500s and repaired in 1713, is the most graceful in Dorset. There was a bridge here at least as early as 1341 and the amount of stone that has been used is an indication of the former importance of these little used lanes.

It spans the Stour just downstream from White Mill and though it is owned by the county rather than the Trust it makes a dominant and delightful backdrop to the view across the meadows. The parapet bulges at the cutwaters and the stone is a mix of grey Purbeck ashlars with blocks of brown gritstone from the Dorset heaths. As with a number of Dorset's older bridges it carries a cast-iron plate, from early last century, with the threat that anyone causing it damage is liable to seven years' transportation.

Legend of Knowlton Bell: "Knowlton bell is stole/ And thrown into White Mill Hole/ Where all the devils in hell/ Could never pull up Knowlton bell."

It was stolen from the church, now ruined, close to the B3078 to the south of

White Mill Bridge: the most graceful mediaeval bridge in Dorset. Knowlton's church bell was thrown into the mill pond on the other side.

Cranborne. As the doggerel implies, the bell is believed to contain supernatural powers that prevented its recovery after the thieves dumped it in the mill pond, from the bridge, because they were being pursued.

On the other hand, spoiling a good story, there are alternative traditions that the bell was raised and put into Shapwick or Sturminster Marshall churches or taken away by a man from Horton, Mr Compton. But given this diversity of thought, why believe them? There is every chance that the verse is the correct memory of events, and Knowlton bell did defy lifting attempts and still lies in the riverbed.

Landscape: A mixture of lowland pastures and arable fields on alluvial gravels in the Stour valley. The Trust intends to prevent any further removal of hedges as, at Shapwick, many of them preserve boundaries of the mediaeval field systems in strips that run at right-angles from the valley lane.

Trust ownership: 1,000 acres, part of lands left to the Trust by Ralph Bankes in 1982.

Location and access: Turn off the B3082, Wimborne to Blandford road, for Shapwick village. The turning is opposite the entrance to Badbury Rings. From Shapwick the lane down the valley, towards Sturminster Marshall, brings you to White Mill and then White Mill Bridge.

Third World Dorset, opposite White Mill: rustic corner, still with 'cown' as they call them. The architecture is the country-modern school; corrugated iron on top of old thatch.

Brownsea islander: one of England's last red squirrels, going home from the beach.

Section 5

Survey of **National Trust properties** in the **Isle of Purbeck**

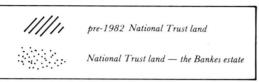

	pre-1982 National Trust land
	National Trust land — the Bankes estate

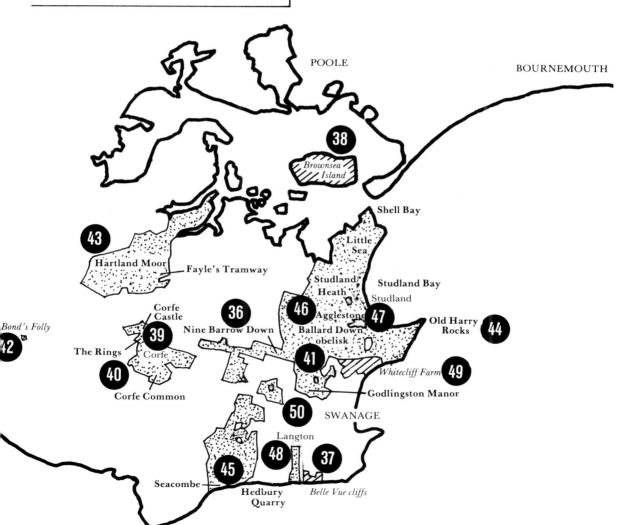

AILWOOD DOWN, NINE BARROW DOWN
and WESTWOOD FARM
between Corfe Castle and Studland   *SZ 000 814*

Neolithic long barrow (SY 997 815): Mound of chalk, 112 feet long by forty feet wide, which would have been built to cover collective burials of the Neolithic period, the Late Stone Age, about 3,500 BC. The barrow, aligned as was usual from west to east (the burial end) is beside later round barrows strung along the skyline at the summit of the Purbeck Hills. This is the only long barrow in the Isle of Purbeck.

Bronze Age round barrows (SY 995 816 to 997 815): The major cemetery of the Purbeck Hills, each mound covering a single burial urn accompanied with aristocratic grave goods and food for the after-life, erected by the Beaker Folk from the Rhine who established the rich warrior-dominated Wessex culture of 2,100 to 1,500 BC. Actually there are seventeen mounds on Ailwood Down (giving their name to Nine Barrow Down which has shifted eastwards on the map), though most are too slight to count. Only nine are over two feet high. They are set in a line running for eight hundred feet along the crest of the Purbeck ridge at six hundred feet above sea level. The largest is a hundred feet in diameter and ten feet high, surrounded by a ditch that is still four feet deep. All received the attention of eighteenth or early nineteenth century barrow diggers – and should have provided above-average plunder – but no record exists.

Legend: That they are the graves of nine kings who were killed in battle.

Landscape: The Trust owns the hog's back of the central Purbeck Hills, from the southern slope of Rollington Hill eastwards, with a tongue of valley land

Ailwood Down: prehistoric burial mounds (above and opposite).

and small fields extending south to Westwood Farm and Harman's Cross. The dry chalky sides of Ailwood Down and Nine Barrow Down are designated by the Nature Conservancy as a site of special scientific interest for negative reasons – the paucity of their flora. This is poor because the escarpment is exposed to the weather and the full scorching heat of the sun. An area of gorse scrub lies beside the barrow group but much of the top of this steep-sided double escarpment has been ploughed for cereals. The view is extensive, across the heath and Poole Harbour and northward to the hills of Cranborne Chase and central Dorset. The Swanage valley, the limestone plateau of southern Purbeck, and the sea are overlooked from the other side.

Trust ownership: 400 acres, part of the Corfe Castle Estate left to the Trust by Ralph Bankes in 1982.

Location and access: Park in the viewpoint car-park on the Corfe Castle to Studland road, the B3351, half a mile to the west of the Golf Course.

Walk around the first corner in the direction of the Golf Course and then cross over to the gate. A track cut in the hillside leads uphill and then follows the left-hand field boundary to the wood where it bends to the right to ascend the slope of the Purbeck Hills.

At the top you continue to the middle of the hill and then turn right along it, towards Corfe Castle. The barrow group is a mile from your car.

BELLE VUE CLIFFS
south of Swanage   *SZ 015 770*

Shipwreck: The rocks at the foot of this cliff stretch eastward towards Round Down and Anvil Point. They are known, descriptively, as the Ragged Rocks

Belle Vue Cliffs: on each side the cliff path follows the clifftop and crosses an old stone wall into the Trust's land. Below (opposite) are the ship-killing Ragged Rocks and a precipitous wall of Purbeck stone that extends in the picture to the 'Halsewell' wreck-site beyond Seacombe. Spot the rock climbers, not that the author noticed them until the book was printing!

and their most horrific death toll was claimed on 29 April 1882.

The Liverpool sailing ship *Alexandrovna* was washed on to these "broken billows which covered the sea with foam for hundreds of yards from the rocks" and all seventy-seven of her crew drowned.   A steamer visit in the sunshine of the following week brought ghouls from Bournemouth and Swanage to witness the scene – naked bodies were visible in various stages of mutilation amongst massive quantities of wreckage.

Landscape: These are solid Purbeck stone cliffs, rising instantly to about a hundred and fifty feet, with unspoilt limestone downland at the top.   The Purbeck stone is still being worked a short distance inland.

Trust ownership: 51 acres, bought in 1976 with a donation from Mr L. Forder in memory of his wife, Mrs E.A.E. Forder.

Location and access: Immediately west of the Durlston Country Park.   Use its car-park.

Turn south along Swanage seafront for almost as far as you can go.   Turn right near the end, up Seymer Road, and then swing leftwards up the hill into Durlston Road.   The Country Park car-park is at the end.

You walk westwards along the coastal path, with your back to the Anvil Point lighthouse, for nearly a mile to the stile in an old stone wall.   This is the boundary between Dorset County Council's Country Park and the National Trust's Belle Vue Cliffs holding.

Brownsea Island: the South West Approaches.

BROWNSEA ISLAND
in Poole Harbour   *SZ 020 880*

Roman Pottery (SZ 032 884): At the north-east corner of the island, 200 feet from the sea wall at the extreme point of the lowest tides, was a Roman pottery kiln. It lies at the extremity of the nature reserve, which has restricted public access. This was one of the Purbeck sites that made black-burnished ware, and perhaps joined with the others in supplying military contracts for the quartermasters of Hadrian's Wall.

Mediaeval hermitage of St Andrew (SZ 028 876): Established by the mediaeval monks of Cerne Abbas, apparently in the area of the farm, 150 yards west of the Castle. Seven burials have been dated to between 1100 and 1230. When Colonel William Waugh built the present church in 1853 he took "particular care to preserve the small portion of the chapel wall which remains". If this is incorporated in St Mary's it is well disguised.

Henry VIII's Castle (SZ 031 876): Built in 1547, this protected the mouth of Poole Harbour from seaborne attack. It was a square single-storey blockhouse with walls forty feet long and nine feet thick, protected on the three landward sides by a moat and with its hexagonal gun platform facing seaward. Most of its stonework is incorporated in the basement of the present eighteenth century Castle. Queen Elizabeth made a present of the island as a gift for life to "a mere vegetable of the Court, that sprang up in the night", one Sir Christopher Hatton.

Brownsea islander: a young razorbill.

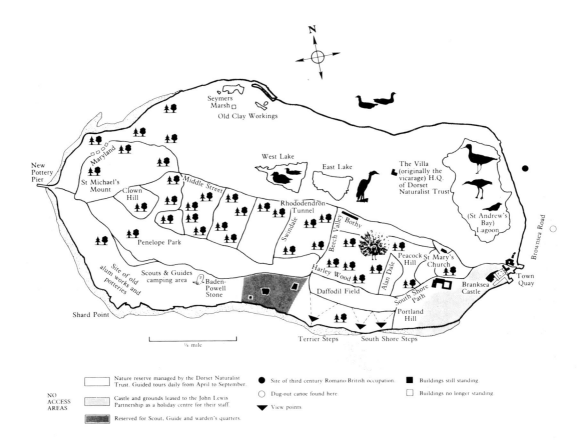

National Trust map of Brownsea Island, which to mix sensible measure with metric is to the scale of ¼ mile = 23 mm (making the island just over a mile and a half long). It shows the wildlife emphasis (Dorset Naturalists' Trust – re-named Dorset Trust for Nature Conservation) and the whiter areas are a nature reserve with access restricted to daily guided tours. This zone includes the freshwater lakes and the saltwater lagoon of St Andrew's Bay.

Alum Mines (SZ 021 875): Common or potash alum, used medically as an astringent and a styptic, was produced on the southern shore of the island in the area of South Shore Lodge and Barnes' Bottom, with the kilns being on a piece of level ground between the bank and the water. Work in the nineteenth century uncovered old cisterns "formed on solid oak staves". The Mayor of Poole protested to Sir Francis Ashley on 4 February 1586 about the drinking habits of James Mounsey and his men "who farmeth the mines of Brownsea".

Shelling of the 'Bountiful Gift': A case of post-Armada nerves in February 1589 caused the Brownsea garrison to open fire on the copperas-carrying barque *Bountiful Gift* as she attempted to leave Poole Harbour. The master, Walter Merritt, and crewman William Drake were killed. The commander of the castle, Walter Partridge, was convicted of manslaughter but pardoned because he had intended only "to stay the sail ship".

Brownsea Island, the Castle: this Gothic mansion has a genuine fortress underneath.

Civil War preparations: Four large guns and several chests of muskets were ferried to Brownsea in February 1645 for a twenty-strong Parliamentary garrison.

Pride's Place: In the Cromwellian period, in 1654, Colonel Thomas Pride was stationed with the Brownsea garrison. His place in English history is 'Pride's Purge', the forceful exclusion of Presbyterians from their seats in the House of Commons on 3rd December 1648. The Brownsea garrison in 1655 captured an intruding vessel which had a commission from James, the second son of Charles I, who later became James II of England.

Monmouth interlude: Charles II and his illegitimate son James, Duke of Monmouth, were rowed around the island on 15th September 1665. They didn't land – because the island was owned by Sir Robert Clayton, to whom Charles owed £30,000. They thought that he too had retreated to the country to escape the plague.

Seventeenth century mansion: Little remains of Sir Robert Clayton's large house, which was in ruin by 1800. There are now only two brick walls and piers supporting a gateway, preserved in the courtyard of an old dairy building west of the Castle.

Copperas manufacture (SZ 021 875): The sixteenth century alum works was re-opened by Sir Robert Clayton to produce a sulphate of iron, known as green

Brownsea Island: the Castle has another castle in its basement. The right-hand slanting wall is that of Henry VIII's gun platform.

Brownsea Island: St Mary's church, built by Colonel William Petrie Waugh in 1853-54. Unfortunately he was speculating, with the money of others.

vitriol, that was used in dyeing, tanning and painting. Celia Fiennes, one of the great female explorers, came to Brownsea in 1698-99 and saw the "great furnaces under" that kept the pans boiling, and the adding of old iron and nails.

Mad Benson's Castle (SZ 031 876): William Benson bought the island in about 1710 from the executors of Sir Robert Clayton and proceeded to add a "great hall" which transformed the old castle, then still crown property, into a country house. He grew rare plants in the mild micro–climate, sponsored Samuel Johnson's Psalms and erected John Milton's monument in Westminster Abbey. For these he was lampooned by Alexander Pope: "On two unequal crutches propp'd he came, Milton's on this, and on that one Johnson's name ..... On poets' tombs see Benson's titles writ." A nervous breakdown followed in 1741 and his love of books turned to hatred. Poole people talked of black masses, necromancy and witchcraft.

Sturt's Castle (SZ 031 876): Humphrey Sturt of Crichel House rebuilt the Castle after 1765, into a four storey tower with wings branching off at all sides.

He spent £50,000 on the island. Arthur Young, the agriculturalist who never missed a trick in propagating the virtues of infertile land, credited Sturt with the planting of a million firs [two thousand to the acre, which sounds a little close] and grass that annually improves: "I never have seen finer clover – thicker, more luxuriant, or that promised better to be most profitable land." He concluded that no production could exceed "what may be found in great plenty on this happy island, which is really England in miniature".

Seymer's House (SZ 018 885): In ruin on the northern shore; built by Sir Charles Chad who held the island until about 1840. Between it and the mid-northern shore are disused clay-mine shafts and pits.

St Andrew's Bay, Maryland Village and the Brownsea Pottery episode (the Bay is at SZ 030 880, the village at SZ 012 882, and the Pottery Works at SZ 013 875): Colonel William Petrie Waugh bought the island in 1852 and gave £13,000, believing it was worth at least £100,000 an acre "for its clay". It wasn't but as Waugh was a director of the London and Eastern Banking Corporation he had no trouble raising an instant £237,000 and spent it in 1853-54 on a million bricks to enclose St Andrew's Bay, the embellishment of the Castle, and building himself St Mary's church – by now he needed God on his side. The Lord doesn't suffer fools, however, and the 1855 development of Brownsea [then Branksea] Pottery and Maryland Village for its clayworkers failed to produce

Brownsea Island, St Mary's church: home comforts in Colonel Waugh's private chapel. Above the fireplace is a fine seventeenth century Italian painting of the Crucifixion.

Brownsea Island, in St Mary's church: effigy and tomb of Charles van Raalte, 1857-1907, and his devoted Florence who would live another twenty years.

Britain's best porcelain and has left us little more than sewer pipes. Thousands of tons of these lie in banks up to eight feet high on the shore opposite the west end of Furzey Island. It is strewn with broken pottery and vitrified bricks for more than four hundred yards. The foundations of Waugh's pottery are in grassland directly opposite the Furzey boathouse. Waugh fled to Spain in 1857 after his deaf wife had received a party of Poole tradesmen who landed to ask if her husband would represent them in Parliament. She responded by asking for time to pay.

St Mary's church (SZ 028 878): Brownsea's church stands near the eastern end of the island, at the edge of the woods, and was built by Colonel William Petrie Waugh in 1853-54. The foundation stone was laid in style, watched by a thousand spectators who had been brought across from Poole in a shuttle service of small boats. It is a pleasant enough piece of Victoriana but the real treasures were imported from London, including the ceiling over the family pew which is said to have come from Crosby Place, Bishopsgate, which was

Opposite, in St Mary's churchyard, Brownsea Island: 'This ancient well-head or pozzo which surmounts the grave of the late Right Honourable George Augustus Frederick Cavendish-Bentinck – brought by him from Italy as a monument of sixteenth century art revival – has been placed here to his memory by his widow and children.' It is carved in pink marble.

THIS ANCIENT WELL HEAD OR POZZO
WHICH SURMOUNTS THE GRAVE OF THE LATE
RIGHT HONOURABLE GEORGE AUGUSTUS FREDERICK
CAVENDISH-BENTINCK — BROUGHT BY HIM FROM
ITALY AS A MONUMENT OF SIXTEENTH CENTURY
ART REVIVAL HAS BEEN PLACED HERE TO HIS MEMORY
BY HIS WIDOW AND CHILDREN

built in 1446. This hall, erected by wool merchant John Crosby, was according to historian John Stow "the highest at that time in London". Later it was the home of Richard III, when he was Duke of Gloucester, and hence the ceiling is a link with the conspiracy to murder the Princes in the Tower. Brownsea's sixteenth century panels also came from London. The pew has a fireplace, eighteenth century candelabrum and a seventeenth century Italian painting of the Crucifixion.

The other Italian objets d'art, including several sixteenth century carvings and a large wrought-iron well-head of the period which is set in the churchyard, were brought here by George Augustus Cavendish-Bentinck, the owner from 1870 to 1890. The well-head is above the family grave. On the south side of the tower is a family chapel that was added as a memorial vault in 1908 for the remains of the next owners, Charles and Florence van Raalte.

The Castle fire: It was gutted on 26 January 1896 whilst the owner, Major Kenneth Balfour MP, was at evensong in the island church. The castle was rebuilt a year later. It now has to be admired from the outside being a holiday home for the John Lewis Partnership and without general public access.

The Island's name – Branksea: Charles van Raalte, the next owner of Brownsea, was a wealthy socialite who narrowly failed to make it into Parliament as a Unionist [Tory] in then-Liberal Poole. His lasting contribution to the story was to change the island's name, in 1903, from Branksea to Brownsea – which was understandable in the circumstances as his weekend guests had a habit of thinking that Branksome Station = Branksea [Branksome Station = Brownsea Island]. Constantly having to search the Poole suburbs for upper class waifs and strays to put on the boat decided him upon the change.

World's first scout camp, 1907 (SZ 016 876): The moment of Brownsea's past that is kept alive is the fact that Robert Baden Powell chose the south-west side of the island for a camp for twenty boys that was his first outdoor experiment with his ideas on scouting. He divided his boys into patrols and for ten days taught them games and treated them as unarmed combatants – the sort of game that he played in Mafeking as the world watched whilst the Boer War was fought and won in other parts of South Africa. The lads were to be: "Trusty, loyal, helpful, brotherly, courteous, kind, obedient, smiling, thrifty, pure as the rustling wind." One wonders where he found them. Their commemorative stone is on the island's southern ridge, overlooking Furzey Island. Baden Powell was one of the first examples of twentieth century marketing though his lasting achievement is the world scouting movement rather than the Mafeking myth.

Florence Bonham Christie's secret island: Enter the dragon, in 1927, with a name sounding like a merger between West End auction rooms. She sacked the loyal van Raalte staff in 1929 and let the island return to nature. Bertha Horthung Olsen threw a visitor into the sea in 1933 and the following year fire devastated all but the eastern end of the island, its smoke clouds reaching France. Peter Scott was declared undesirable; media attention was discouraged and in Poole they talked of spies and rats as big as cats.

Brownsea Island: commemorative stone to Baden-Powell and the world's first scout camp. The view is south and sunny – Old Harry Rocks are glimpsed on the left.

Clearing station for Aliens: Thousands of Dutch refugees were isolated, questioned and cleared through Brownsea.   This armada of small boats put to sea after the Germans smashed into the Low Countries on 10 May 1940 and was shepherded to Brownsea by the Royal Navy.

1940 Fortifications: Two six-inch naval guns were mounted on Battery Point, the island's ancient site for a gun emplacement, to guard the entrance to Poole Harbour.   The 347th Battery of 554th Coast Regiment of the Royal Artillery proceeded to eat the island's peacock, reviving a military tradition going back to Alexander the Great.

Major strategic night decoy, 1941-44   (SZ 012 881):   Rows of large wire baskets, courtesy of the pyrotechnic department at Elstree Studios, were constructed at the west end of the island.   They were filled with wood shavings sodden with paraffin and ignited to simulate burning buildings.   A bath tub and lavatory cistern flooded them with water to produce a white-hot flash, just like a bomb bursting.   This drew the German bombers from Poole and Bournemouth. The best documented example was on 22 May 1942 when the initial enemy flares dropped on Poole were extinguished in time for Brownsea to come alive and then rock with countless explosions.   In all it saved the Bournemouth conurbation from a thousand tons of German bombs, which is of some personal interest as my parents were among those who would otherwise have received them.

Brownsea Island: crenellated Victoriana on the public quayside.

Brownsea Island: ditto, at the private landing stage for the Castle.

Brownsea Island: background, centre – the Quay to which the island's ferry services bring visitors from Poole Quay and Sandbanks. Foreground – island warden Alan Bromby and a contrivance on rails that is used to ground a boat, so that her bottom is exposed for attention.

Post-war obscurity: Mrs Christie became a total recluse, retreating to a couple of rooms in the Castle, until her death in 1961 at the age of ninety-eight. The time-capsule passed to the National Trust for re-opening to the world.

Demolition of Maryland village (SZ 012 882): Five ruined terraces, each of four pottery workers' cottages, built in 1855 at the north-west corner of the island – known as Maryland village – were demolished by the National Trust in 1963. They had been named for Colonel William Waugh's wife, Mary.

Dorset Trust for Nature Conservation reserve (north of a line from SZ 017 883 to SZ 032 878): 200 acres of the northern half of the island has access restricted to small accompanied parties as it is a wildlife refuge. The area is fenced off, to the north of the island's main central trackway, Middle Street. Brownsea has one of the last populations of the rare native red squirrel in southern England. About a hundred survive. The heronry above the lakes in the centre of the northern woods has around a hundred nests, and is the second largest in Britain. St Andrew's Bay, to the north of the main track from the Castle to the church – an area which Colonel Waugh temporarily drained in 1853 – now supports one of only three sandwich terneries on the South Coast. The

Brownsea Island: the former Vicarage. This fine Victorian villa is now the island headquarters for the Dorset Trust for Nature Conservation.

common tern also nests there.   More oystercatchers nest on Brownsea than anywhere else in Dorset or Hampshire.   Hedgehogs are found on the island and even Sika deer, whose ancestors swam back across from the Rempstone pine forest to re-establish a colony that had been introduced in 1896.   Peacock are popular with the visitors, to the extent that notices have to be erected asking them to desist from plucking feathers.

Landscape: Oval-shaped island with a low sandy ridge along its spine, covered with dense pine woods in the central and northern parts.   The hot sandy southern slopes are largely heath and grass.   Shallow safe bathing off the south side.   I have written a separate descriptive history of the island; *Brownsea: Dorset's Fantasy Island* [1986].

Trust ownership: 500 acres, presented to the Treasury by John Bonham Christie, in lieu of estate duties after his grandmother's death on 28 April 1961; handed over to the Trust by the National Land Fund procedure in 1962.

Location and access: In the middle of Poole Harbour, served by ferries from Poole Quay and Sandbanks from the start of April to the end of September – or by your own boat to Pottery Pier at the west end of the island.   Those arriving by ferry should check the time of the last return boat before they disperse into the island.

Brownsea Island: the ruins of a small building near Seymer's House, with an ant nest (detail below) on the old bath beside the door.

Brownsea Island: the West Lake, inside the wildlife reserve managed by the Dorset Trust for Nature Conservation.

Brownsea Island: detritus on the north-west shore.

Brownsea Island: Cavendish Road through the nature reserve pines.

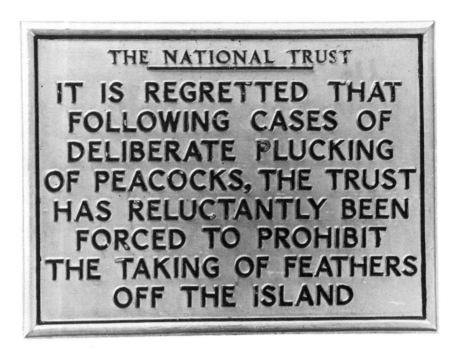

THE NATIONAL TRUST

IT IS REGRETTED THAT FOLLOWING CASES OF DELIBERATE PLUCKING OF PEACOCKS, THE TRUST HAS RELUCTANTLY BEEN FORCED TO PROHIBIT THE TAKING OF FEATHERS OFF THE ISLAND

Brownsea Island: look stranger, wherever you may travel in this galaxy observe the same rule – take only photographs, and leave only footprints.

CORFE CASTLE
overlooking Corfe Castle village   *SY 959 823*

Old Hall: Herring-bone walling and the windows of a Conquest period hall, on the site of the previous Saxon royal house, pre-date the rest of the ruins at Corfe Castle.   This masonry can be found between the Butavant Tower and the South Tower on the south side of the West Bailey.   At the entrance to the West Bailey the later South-west Gatehouse [the one beside the Keep] is known as Edward's Gate.   Tradition holds that it was built on the spot where seventeen-year-old Edward, King of England, was assassinated by members of his step-mother's household on 15 April 978.   He was knifed in the back.

Norman Keep: The great central keep at Corfe, which despite demolitions still partly stands to eighty feet high, was started about 1095 and completed by around 1105.   It is one of the earliest mediaeval fortresses in Britain.

Corfe Castle from the Church Knowle road: the West Bailey is the near part.

West Bailey (around the site of the Old Hall):   This was fortified with its three towers in 1201-04, when Corfe Castle was King John's state prison.   In 1202 its dungeon held Savaris de Mauléon, a baron from Poitou on the edge of the disputed Aquitaine.   He had taken John's mother, Eleanor, prisoner at Vienne.   John rescued her.   Of the twenty-five French prisoners held at Corfe "where there was never food nor drink" most starved to death, though Savaris was "turned" as we would say in telespeak – he returned to France as a British agent and became a famous troubadour.

The Great Ditch: The deep ditch between the Keep and the vulnerable Outer Bailey was quarried out of the hill in 1207 when John made Corfe his treasury for the store of confiscated church funds and other finances for the coming war against France.   A great convoy of carts was needed to move the cash to Portsmouth in 1214.

King's Hall and John's state rooms: Known as the 'Gloriette', these start to the east of the Keep and were built between 1205-08.   The east wall still stands to two storeys and has pointed-arched windows in elaborately mullioned stone. King John enjoyed hunting in Purbeck, where he could also keep an eye on his money.

Outer Bailey: Timber palisades around the Outer Bailey were replaced in stone after 1212 but the main perimeter defences date from the second half of the thirteenth century – the First Tower, South-west Gatehouse, Plukenet Tower, Horseshoe Tower, Outer Gatehouse and the Outer Bridge.

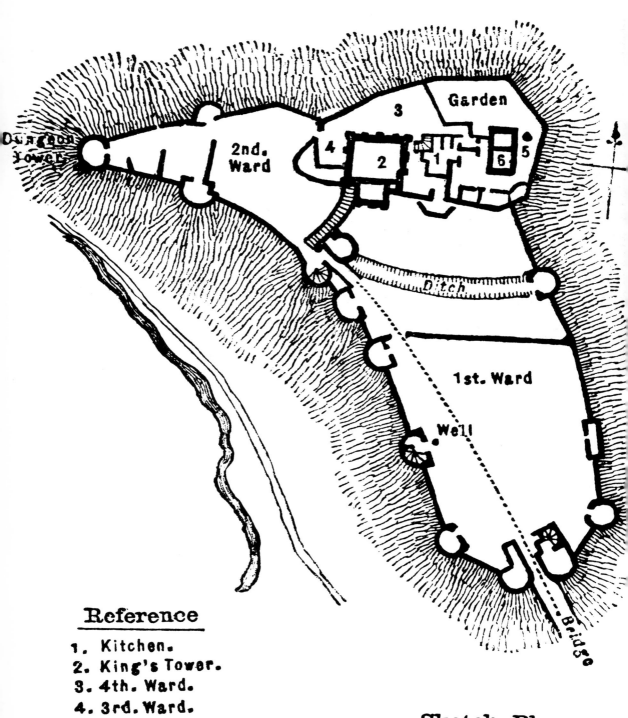

Garden

3

2nd.
Ward

Dungeon
Tower

4

2

1

6 5

Ditch

1st. Ward

Well

Bridge

Reference

1. Kitchen.
2. King's Tower.
3. 4th. Ward.
4. 3rd. Ward.
5. Well.
6. Queen's Tower.

Sketch Plan
of
CORFE CASTLE

Corfe Castle from West Hill: from the left edge of the page as you look at the plan opposite. The closest bit, the Dungeon Tower, alias the Butavant Tower, collapsed down the slope in a gale on 11 July 1866. The remainder of the destruction was ordered by Parliament, on 4 March 1646.

Siege and destruction: Having survived an abortive siege in 1139 when King Stephen failed to oust one of his barons, Baldwin de Redvers, history caught up with Corfe in the Civil War between King Charles and his Parliament.   In 1643, a troop of Parliamentary horsemen tried to use Purbeck's traditional May Day stag hunt as a pretext for entering Corfe Castle.   Lady Mary Bankes had the gates shut against them and until 1646 Corfe was unsuccessfully besieged as the Civil War ebbed and flowed across the English countryside from Marston Moor to Naseby Field.   Somerset fell to Fairfax's cavalry in 1645 and by 1646 the castles at Corfe and Portland were the only token royalist garrisons holed-up in Dorset.   A royalist officer at Corfe, Lieutenant Colonel Thomas Pittman, conspired to allow a disguised group of the enemy into Corfe.   They ended the last forty-eight day siege at 8 am on 27 February 1646 when the Governor, Colonel Henry Anketell, surrendered.   His men were caught in impossible crossfire between the intruders inside and the other attackers outside.   On 4 March 1646 the House of Commons ordered the demolition of Corfe, which was no easy task and reducing it to ruin took several months. Some of the undermined masonry slipped down the sides in the subsequent centuries.

East Street and Corfe Castle.

Landscape: The Castle Hill lies between two streams of the Corfe River, known locally as the Byle and the Wicken, which have cut the only break in the central massif of the Purbeck Hills. The strategic position is superb, commanding the passes on each side, and the visual splendour of the ruins is the equal of anything in Europe. In places the ivy will be retained and gardened by the Trust "to maintain and enhance the romantic quality of the castle". There is a much fuller history of the castle in my book on *Exploring the Heartland of Purbeck* [1986].

Trust ownership: 60 acres, being the heart of the Corfe Castle Estate left to the Trust by Ralph Bankes [*see the Kingston Lacy entry*] in 1982. It had come into his family in 1635. Corfe Castle was then acquired by Sir John Bankes, the Attorney-General to Charles I, whose wife, Mary, defended it in the Civil War. The Trust's long-term aim with regard to its other properties in Corfe Castle is to acquire ownership over all the properties in The Square but to sell other properties in the village that are surplus to requirements.

Location and access: Corfe Castle has been attracting 170,000 visitors a year. The car-park is in the village; turn off the main road into the Square and then left into West Street. The car-park is signposted on the right, after the low terraces of stone-roofed cottages. From March to the end of October the castle is open daily but in the winter months access is restricted to Saturday and Sunday afternoons.

The Square at Corfe Castle: it is the National Trust's long-term aim to acquire all the properties here, but to dispose of surplus cottages elsewhere in the village.

CORFE COMMON, THE RINGS, WEST HAWES and WEST HILL
south and west of Corfe Castle   *SY 957 817*

Bronze Age round barrows (single barrow at SY 954 824 and a line of them from SY 956 810 to 966 808): There is a skyline burial mound at the end of West Hill, with one of the finest views over Corfe Castle ruins and village. The other barrows on the Trust's lands at Corfe Castle are in a line straddling the bracken covered ridge across the centre of Corfe Common.

Eight, dating from about 2,100 to 1,700 BC, are of varying sizes, from two to eight feet high, and have suffered some disturbance though their contents are unknown.

Celtic fields (SY 957 808): A small group of ancient fields, covering about fifteen acres, lie on the south-facing slope of the western part of the sandy ridge that crosses Corfe Common. The lynchets, which were cultivation terraces, are about eight feet high.

Though not scientifically dated they are probably prehistoric or Romano-British.

The Rings (SY 956 820): An earthen ring-and-bailey siege work, The Rings was constructed in 1139 by King Stephen, the last of the Norman line. His reign had disintegrated to anarchy and in Dorset he failed to oust Baldwin de Redvers, the first Earl of Devon, from Corfe Castle. The castle stands three hundred yards to the north-east.

"When traitors perceived that he was a mild man, and soft and good," a chronicler wrote of Stephen, "every powerful man made his castles, and held them against him."

The Rings lie on the first hillock from Corfe Castle, beside the Church Knowle road, and were placed on the side of the slope that tilts away from the Castle hill – so that the activities of the besiegers were less obvious to watchers on the battlements.

Cromwell's Battery was the name of The Rings until the nineteenth century, because it was purpose-built for reoccupation by Parliamentary forces for their camp and artillery emplacement in the Civil War of the 1640s. A gun ramp was cut into the north-east side.

Mediaeval sledge-tracks (SY 958 808): Deep cuttings gouged through the sandy ridge at the centre of Corfe Common date from the Middle Ages when sledges laden with marble were hauled across the common from the quarrylands of southern Purbeck. They were destined for the workshops in Corfe village and the export wharf, Ower Quay on Poole Harbour, from which the ecclesiastical building stone and effigies were shipped to London and the country's principal cathedrals and abbeys.

West Hawes strip fields and mere-stones (SY 958 817): On the west side of the main village car-park at Corfe Castle [off West Street, about midway along] some twenty mediaeval strip fields can be traced in the grass. They are in parallel lines running down the slope to the Corfe River.

The fields are about forty feet wide and up to a hundred and fifty feet long.

Cross into the present fields by the stone stile at the side of the car-park and search out some of the ownership stones – called mere-stones [mere = boundary] – which are like miniature gravestones and carry initials, including "C.C.C.", "N.B." and "R.B."

Landscape: Corfe's immediate countryside comprises two very different landscapes. Northwards is the chalk ridge of the Purbeck Hills and to the south the village stretches into the Wealden sands.

The chalk hills were used for sheep grazing and the indifferent soils to the south for rough grazing for cattle and horses. This is still the case as the bracken covered marginal land continues to be collectively grazed by those holding rights in common to turn out specified numbers of animals. These are passed on with their properties. Notices point out that non-qualifying stock can be impounded.

Trust ownership: 500 acres, surrounding Corfe Castle village, were left to the Trust by Ralph Bankes in 1982.

Corfe Common: shared grazing rights exercised in the bracken.

Location and access: Park in the village car-park at Corfe Castle.   Turn off the main road into The Square and then left into West Street.   The car-park is around the next corner, its entrance signposted between stone-built houses on the right-hand side, and from it public paths lead northwards and westwards.

These paths lead to West Hawes, The Rings, and West Hill.   From the south end of West Street there is a road and several tracks that fan out across Corfe Common.

GODLINGSTON HILL, GODLINGSTON MANOR, SWANAGE BRICK WORKS, ULWELL GAP and BALLARD DOWN OBELISK
between Swanage and Studland   *SZ 013 810*

Giant's Grave (SZ 012 811), Giant's Trencher (SZ 013 811), another barrow on Godlingston Hill (SZ 014 813), and the Ulwell Barrow (SZ 022 813) : Despite their 'Giant' names, the first two mounds are low and small, at the head of the dry coombe on the 500 foot contour on the side of Godlingston Hill. They are indeed of note only for their names as the Victorian excavator John Austen opened both in the 1850s but found nothing.   The other Godlingston Hill barrow, on the northern spur two hundred yards to the north-east of the named barrows, covered a Bronze Age cremation that was sandwiched between two stones.   The six feet high Ulwell Barrow, beneath the obelisk at the west end of Ballard Down, is more interesting, as John Austen dug it in 1857 to reveal a trussed-up skeleton in a chalk-cut grave, with a fine red-ware handled cup which would have held a drink for the journey to the after-world, and an antler in its filling showed how the grave had been dug.   There was another, later, skeleton inserted into the mound as well as urn fragments and a cremation beneath a stone.   Date, about 1,800 to 1,500 BC.

Godlingston Manor (SZ 015 803):   Dating from about 1300 this privately occupied farmhouse is the oldest inhabited building in Swanage parish, and one of the most ancient in Purbeck.   It is at the back of Ulwell – down the western lane [Washpond Lane], four hundred yards beyond the cemetery.   A public path runs along its southern frontage.   The rounded tower at the west end has walls five feet thick; showing this was the family's fortified refuge as enough remains of contemporary walling to prove that their house had much the same plan as the present manor.

It was in "a sad state of dilapidation" in 1867 and threatened with demolition.

Godlingston Manor:
ancient fortified tower at left.

Ulwell Barrow, a prehistoric burial mound: with the ex-London Ballard Down Obelisk thrusting from its side.

Ballard Down Obelisk (SZ 022 813): The twenty-three feet high obelisk above the Ulwell Gap on the landward side of Ballard Down is a former London gas-lamp which stood outside the church of St Mary Woolnoth on the corner of King William Street and Lombard Street in the City. It was re-erected here by George Burt in 1892 to commemorate the Swanage Water Act. Water was first tapped from the chalk formation in 1884 and two stone plaques record these events; the reservoir and pumping station are to the south. The white Cornish marble lamp collapsed soon after erection but was rebuilt and next taken down in 1940 when it was regarded as a navigation aid for German bombers. In 1973, through the efforts of Bishop George Snow and the Royal Engineers, it was put back up again though there were difficulties with one six-foot section which had to be left beside the plinth. The gas pipe can be seen running through the centre.

Swanage Brick Works: Near the cemetery, beside Ulwell's western lanes, stand the sheds, kilns and chimneys of the Swanage Brick and Tile Company Ltd, at the edge of the Trust's lands. They are a living example of industrial archaeology, being one of the few works in Britain that still produce hand-made bricks. These are shaped in several distinct shades and textures, using the nearby Wealden beds and their red, purple, brown, blue and green clays. The mix includes white, blue, brown and grey sands and the materials are

Ballard Down Obelisk (opposite) with Swanage behind; and (above) in cross-section. This 'missing' segment stands at its side and betrays the monument's original function – it has a gas-pipe through the centre.

weathered for months before the bricks are thrown. So personal is the moulding technique that the workers know just who made a particular brick from the pattern of its creases. For a week a brick is gently dried and loses a pint of water by evaporation. Then 45,000 bricks are stacked in the kiln and fired for 85 hours, using three thousand gallons of oil, at a temperature of 1200 degrees celsius. The kilns take ten days to cool. The colour of the brick depends upon its position in the kiln – rather than the ingredients – and the Dorset Blue variety which is specified by architects for prestige work comes from the hottest part of the kiln. Light reds predominate towards the bottom.

Landscape: The Ulwell Gap is a dry cutting through the chalk ridge of the Purbeck Hills, with steep escarpments rising from two hundred feet to 550 feet on the east side and 654 feet on the west. It is a dramatic landscape with fine views over the Swanage valley to the south and Godlingston Heath, Studland and Poole Harbour to the north. The Trust's lands around Ulwell are featured in my book on *Old Swanage* [1983].

Trust ownership: 500 acres, part of the Corfe Castle Estate left to the Trust by Ralph Bankes in 1982.

Location and access: The Studland to Swanage road passes through the Ulwell Gap and public paths lead off into the hills. Turn off at Ulwell for Godlingston

Kilns of the Swanage Brick and Tile Company Ltd at Godlingston: stacks of hand-made bricks in the foreground.

Manor, along either of the lanes that go off to the south–west.

In half a mile you pass Swanage Brick Works, to the right, and then the cemetery on the left-hand side. The next group of buildings, to the right, are Godlingston Manor. There are two dirt tracks on the Swanage side of the farm and both are public paths. They take you immediately beside the venerable stone frontage of the manor house, but there is no public access to the interior or elsewhere in the grounds.

GRANGE ARCH, known locally as BOND'S FOLLY
near Kimmeridge   *SY 912 818*

The physical folly: An "eye-catcher" designed to appear above the trees of the Great Wood at Creech as a castle silhouetted on the skyline of the Purbeck Hills, when viewed from the Grange country house below. In reverse, from the hill, the view is framed by the stone arch. The single length of wall of grey Purbeck stone is castellated and studded with little pyramids. It was built by Denis Bond, the owner of Creech Grange 1706-46.

The intellectual folly: Since I started writing about Purbeck in the Dorset County Magazine at the end of the 1960s I have done my best to keep alive the local name, Bond's Folly, as it was in danger of being completely eclipsed by

Grange Arch was Bond's picturesque folly: his political folly was insider-dealing with state lands and it got him expelled from the House of Commons.

the Ordnance Survey's insistence – as a sop to a former landowner of the Grange – on the less revealing "Grange Arch". The reason for the family's embarrassment was that "Bond's Folly" had a double meaning and would originally have been used with a chuckle. For Denis Bond's folly in life was not this arch but the major corruption scandal of the 1720s when he was expelled from the House of Commons, where he sat as a member for Poole, for "fraudulently and clandestinely" contracting to sell for less than they were worth the state-owned lands in the Lake District.

Landscape: Outstanding views from 625 feet, over heathland and the Frome valley; including the steaming reactors of Winfrith atomic research station and the town of Wareham as well as Poole Harbour. The Steeple area is featured in my *Guide to Purbeck Coast and Shipwreck* [1984]; the adjoining army ranges in *Lulworth and Tyneham Revisited* [1985]; the clay lands to the north are described in *Purbeck's Heath* [1987].

Trust ownership: 1 acre, given by J. W. G. Bond in 1942.

Location and access: Four miles south of Wareham. Turn off the A351 at Stoborough, on the road to Kimmeridge. Climb to the top of the Purbeck Hills and park in the Creech picnic area on the brow of the hill. Walk eastwards [away from the army range red flags] for a mile along the prehistoric ridgeway which survives as an attractive green lane along the hog's back of the Purbeck Hills.

HARTLAND MOOR NATIONAL NATURE RESERVE, MIDDLEBERE PENINSULA, SHARFORD BRIDGE, SCOTLAND FARM and NEW MILLS HEATH
between Wareham and Corfe Castle SY 950 850

Sharford Bridge (SY 967 847): Packhorse bridge over the Corfe River, reached by a bridleway eastwards from the southern edge of Hartland Moor. It is stone built with two arches and probably dates from the sixteenth century as it is shown as "Sherford Bridge" on John Speed's map of 1610.

John Speed's map, 1610: 'Sherford bridge' is just up from the initial letter of 'Purbeck'.

On the other side of the river, which is a densely overgrown trickle in most summers, the track leads through the conifer plantations to Bushey.

Hartland Moor: the best bog in Dorset. It looks, and is, a long way from the bridge at Slepe to Creech Barrow and the Purbeck Hills. Occupants en route in midsummer include marsh orchids (opposite) which are as spectacular a flowering plant as Britain produces.

Scotland Farm (SY 962 840): Lying at the edge of New Mills Heath, this was built by William Whefer with large blocks of ashlar that must have come from the ruins of Corfe Castle. There is a 1665 date-stone; two decades after its destruction. Stone slates cover the roof and the solidly built single-storey building has attic rooms, stone mullioned windows, chimney stacks at either end, and an attractive stone porch. The barn and geese complete an olde worlde farmyard setting, which has the distinction of having been painted by Gordon Beningfield.

Fayle's Tramway (originally called the New Line, to distinguish it from the previous cart track, SY 947 833 to 970 865): Benjamin Fayle laid a horse-drawn tramway – Dorset's first railway – from his clay-pits at Norden across Langton Wallis Heath, and the southern parts of Middlebere Heath and Hartland Moor to a jetty on an inlet of Poole Harbour 700 yards east of Middlebere Farm. Production rose as a result from 14,500 tons of clay in 1802 to 22,000 tons in 1808: "The clay is conveyed on small carriages with four wheels, carrying two tons each. Three horses draw ten tons to the sea-side three times a day, at the expense of about sixpence dead-weight." The gently downhill incline is in wide curves through low cuttings. The gauge was 3 feet 9 inches. The rails had an L-shaped flange [nowadays the flange would be on the wheels]. The surviving sleepers at Middlebere weigh about 70 lbs and are 18 inches square and 9 inches deep, being set in two separate rows rather than crossing the trackbed in the normal fashion.

This splendid rarity of industrial archaeology was completely overlooked by the Royal Commission on Historical Monuments when they surveyed Purbeck. I have provided a full description in my book on *Purbeck's Heath* [1987].

Landscape: Hartland Moor is Purbeck's giant sponge, an acid bog with tracts of the Dorset heath, *Erica ciliaris* – a bell-heather with rosy-purple flowers in late summer when the moor is relatively dry. In early autumn the brilliant blue flowers are the marsh gentians, *Gentiana pneumonanthe*. All three British species of sundew, *Drosera rotundifolia, D. anglica,* and *D. longifolia* are found on this wet heath. The land dips to the North ending with a peninsula of meadowland that juts as another bog, this time of *Spartina* cord-grass, into the shallows of Poole Harbour.

Trust ownership: 1,000 acres, 640 of which are leased to the Nature Conservancy for a National Nature Reserve. This was established in 1954 and extended later. Part of the Corfe Castle Estate left to the Trust by Ralph Bankes in 1982.

Location and access: Turn north off the A351 Wareham to Corfe road at Norden, half a mile from Corfe Castle. Scotland Farm lies in a mile, a hundred yards to the right of the lane, with access along a public footpath. The road then continues across the northern edge of Hartland Moor but here there is only restricted access. A track on the right, just before the bridge leads to Middlebere.

Scotland Farm: 1665, re-using stones from Corfe Castle.

Sharford Bridge: of less importance than when John Speed put it on his map.

OLD HARRY ROCKS, HANDFAST POINT, TURF RICK ROCK, THE PINNACLE, KING BARROW, STUDLAND CASTLE (lost), PARSON'S BARN, FORT HENRY and BALLARD CLIFF

between Studland and Swanage   _SZ 055 824_

Landforms – the chalk stacks   (SZ 056 825):   Sea erosion at Old Harry Rocks is constantly cutting separate blocks of chalk, called 'stacks', which become detached from the parent cliff.   The slender one at the end of The Foreland or Handfast Point, the eastern extremity of the Isle of Purbeck, is Old Harry and he had a plump wife until she drowned in the 1898 gale that destroyed the old chain pier at Brighton.

The devil by any other name: Old Harry was the Devil, and appropriately the main clifftop beside him is known as Old Nick's Ground.   The detached cliff between the coastal path and Old Harry is called No Man's Land.   The gap between it an the mainland is Saint Lucas Leap, reputedly taking its name from a pedigree greyhound that didn't quite make the jump when coursing a hare. Collectively these are Old Harry Rocks, though the headland is also known to the map-makers (though to no one else) as The Foreland or Handfast Point.

The two other detached rocks, to the south towards Ballard Point, are Turf Rick Rock [locally known as The Haystack] and The Pinnacle.   Both are named for their shapes.   The big sea-cave between them is Parson's Barn [*see its entry below*].

King Barrow   (SZ 046 820):   A Bronze Age round barrow, a burial mound of about 1,800 BC, that is forty-five feet in diameter and four feet high.   It lies at the centre of the peninsula, between Studland village and Ballard Down, in an unploughed corner two hundred and fifty yards east of the Warren Wood. The mound has been opened at the centre, but the results went unrecorded.

Another barrow, since destroyed, was known as the Cracker Barrow and stood to the west of the Glebeland Estate at map reference SZ 035 817.

Studland Castle   (lost, at SZ 056 826):   Until about 1770, Studland Castle jutted north-eastwards from the present Old Harry Rocks.   It was a blockhouse, one of Henry VIII's series of coastal forts built about 1540 for heavy guns to protect England from continental retaliation after the king had split from the Roman Catholic church.

It was built with low stone walls, with a slanting angle or 'batter', to withstand the new age of gunpowder.   A second castle was constructed at the eastern end of Brownsea Island [*see its entry*] and together they guarded the approaches to the mouth of Poole Harbour.

Studland Castle was sited next to an earlier castle "upon which it abuteth". Both Studland castles have been claimed by the sea but there must be some stonework surviving in the rock pools.

Parson's Barn smugglers' cave   (SZ 053 823):   Accessible only by boat, the big sea-cave between Turf Rick Rock and The Pinnacle was used by smugglers in the eighteenth and nineteenth centuries.

It takes its name from its spaciousness because in the days of tithes there was nothing more accommodating than the Parson's Barn.   Nor was there a category of person more appreciative of the fact that stolen waters were sweet.

Fort Henry (opposite): sycamores obscure the slit from which Churchill, Eisenhower and Montgomery watched the rehearsals for the Normandy landings, spring 1944.

The landward side of Fort Henry and (opposite) a chalk stack, The Pinnacle.

Fort Henry (SZ 038 828):   The great Fort Henry observation post is in the sycamore trees at the top of Redend Point at the southern end of Studland beach.   It is off the public path system though the National Trust is investigating the possibilities of public access to it.

The bunker was built by Canadian engineers in 1943 and can be glimpsed end-on if you look to the left of the pine trees that stand to your right as you descend the steps on to Studland beach from the Middle Beach car-park.

It is one of Britain's most important relics of the Second World War, being an immense concrete structure ninety feet long with an eye-level observation slit recessed into its almost three feet thick walls for a length of more than eighty feet.   Here stood Winston Churchill, Bernard Montgomery and Dwight D. Eisenhower in the spring of 1944 as they watched live explosions provide reality to Exercise Smash which assaulted the Studland sands in major rehearsals for the launching of the Second Front on to the shores of Normandy.

There is a detailed account of this activity in my book on *Dorset's War 1939-45* [1986].

Ballard Cliff wartime radar and gun-laying posts (SZ 044 813):   There is the site of a rifle range on the downland at the top of Ballard Cliff, the headland at the northern end of Swanage Bay, and concrete footings show the site of what seems to have been a Royal Air Force coastal radar station.

In 1940-41 there was also a Royal Artillery observation post at the seaward end of Ballard Down, for gun-laying which directed the fall of shot from two

sixteen-inch railway mounted howitzers which were concealed in sidings on the heath at Furzebrook, to the north-west of Corfe Castle, as part of the anti-invasion defences.

Ashes of H.G. Wells: The ashes of Herbert George Wells [1866-1946], the radical author and futurist, were scattered from a boat into the sea off Old Harry Rocks.

It seemed appropriate as a passage from his work that was read at the memorial service had concluded: "We are all things that make and pass, striving upon a hidden mission, out to the open sea."

Landscape: The area of headland described in this entry is the eastern peninsula of the Purbeck chalklands.   It projects into Poole Bay and forms a backdrop of white cliffs to both Studland and Swanage bays.

The views are to Bournemouth and the Isle of Wight.   Redend Point, at the south end of Studland's main beach, is an outcrop of gritty sandstone of the Bagshot beds and has visible layers of grey ball clay which cause sticky patches on the shoreline.   There are many old prints and pictures of this spectacular stretch of coast in my *Guide to Purbeck Coast and Shipwreck* [1984].

The Pinnacle, The Haystack, and a chunk of mainland Purbeck.

Old Harry Rocks: the white smudges are gulls in flight during a time exposure, between the yachts.

Trust ownership: 600 acres, part of the Corfe Castle Estate, left to the Trust by Ralph Bankes in 1982.

Location and access: The coastal footpath from Studland to Swanage follows the clifftop of the peninsula to Old Harry Rocks [one mile] and Ballard Cliff [two miles].

Park in Studland village at the Middle Beach car-park. Take the lane southwards beside the Manor House Hotel. It becomes a track. Take note that access to Studland often has to be fought for; an early start is essential on hot summer weekends or you'll find the police have closed the road from Corfe Castle because of overcrowding.

The alternative is to follow the access details given in the Ballard Down entry. Ballard Cliff immediately adjoins this holding and Old Harry Rocks are a mile further along the path, to the north.

SEACOMBE BOTTOM, HEDBURY, ACTON QUARRIES, EASTINGTON FARM, and the PRIEST'S WAY
south-east of Worth Matravers   *SY 984 767*

Priest's Way (SY 979 778 to SY 997 779): The Trust's mile of this ancient highway between Worth Matravers and Swanage is a wide droveway between stone walls. Its name dates back to the early Middle Ages when Swanage [or Sandwich] was a chapelry of Worth parish church and the priest had to trek between the two. As a road, however, it goes back to prehistoric times.

Seacombe Quarries (SY 984 766): These were the most fulsome veins of workable stone on the Purbeck coast and they have been fully exploited, leaving gaping galleries sliced into the western cliff at Seacombe Bottom and running under the hill and along the valley side. Here the stone is 'Portland' rather than Purbeck, taken out in blocks of fifteen tons, and the roofs in the quarries are up to twelve feet high. They are supported by a few huge pillars but inevitably there are rockfalls. Their makers never intended the galleries to stand for centuries and it is unsafe to wander about underground; even with a hard-hat as that would only give cosmetic protection.

These great quarries were in use from about 1700 to 1930 and there were Second World War clearances of spoil for runway hardcore to build the series of military aerodromes across the heathlands of the New Forest.

The 'Halsewell' disaster, 1786 (SY 983 765): The *Halsewell* East Indiaman, outward bound from London for Bengal, was wrecked off Seacombe in a blizzard on 6 January 1786. The 758-ton ship was dashed to pieces, though intrepid quarrymen were later able to salvage cupboards, an hour-glass and other fittings. Captain Richard Pierce drowned with his two daughters and two nieces, five other young ladies, and most of the officers and crew. A total of 168 lives were lost.

There was, however, a daring rescue. Eighty-two men were hauled to safety up the cliffs by quarrymen. The seamen had struggled on to a slanting stone since known as the Halsewell Rock [at the west edge of the Trust's lands, a short distance towards Winspit] and were pulled on to a ledge halfway up the cliff. This shelf was later called the Halsewell Quarry.

The site of the disaster is below the Halsewell Stile at the limits of the Trust's property along the coastal path, at the top of the precipitous cliff that continues westwards to Winspit.

It must be emphasised that not only is there no access to the quarry or the rock, either from the cliff or the shore, but it is exceedingly dangerous even to attempt a closer look.

Seacombe's 'Halsewell' graves (SY 985 767): The site of these, on the other hand, is accessible; though the cannon that marked them have disappeared. Oliver W. Farrer wrote in *Purbeck Papers* in 1858:

"One other sad memorial remains; on the little path of flat grass where the cliffs divide, and the stream, when there is a stream, falls over the cliff, may yet be seen the traces of four long graves. The spot is appropriate. As you stand by the almost obliterated mounds, the eye wanders over little but sea and sky, and the wild solitude of the spot accords with the sadness of the tragedy here played out."

Digging took place in 1972, in an attempt to uncover the graves, but it is hoped that the National Trust will forbid any further pseudo-intellectual curiosity. The dead have a right to some peace.

Hedbury Quarry cannon (SY 993 767): The name derives from the Eidbury family who began the quarry in the eighteenth century. Annoyingly, the

Down and up views of Seacombe Bottom: the 'Halsewell' graves were in the flat ground at the centre of the lower picture.

Hedbury Quarry: seaward cannon and landward winch stone.

Ordnance Survey refuses to name it – even on the large scale maps – but it is a large and conspicuous hole shelved out of the cliffs. Hedbury Quarry lies about half a mile east from Seacombe in the direction of Dancing Ledge and the coastal footpath detours around the top of it.

In 1960 I clambered around the quarry floor and found a twelve-pounder cannon of the Napoleonic period wedged between large blocks of semi-cut stone. The cannon was hauled out and re-set on a stone plinth, pointing seawards, in the mid 1970s. There is some ironwork on the cliff-edge that shows the site of the 'whim', as the quarrymen called the crane that was used to lower cut stone into the boats that took it to Swanage. There was no roadway out of the quarry.

Seacombe's gun-nest (SY 986 768): On the side of the eastern slopes overlooking Seacombe Bottom is a rounded metal turret which is often mistaken for the cockpit of a crashed aircraft. It was in fact put there in 1940, for a single machine-gunner who had the unenviable task of keeping watch on Seacombe in the months when invasion was a real threat. The gun would have been fired from the shuttered front which was the only opening into the canopy – the gunner had no back door from the war.

Invasion 1940: gun-nest on the east side of Seacombe Bottom with the gunner's view (below) over Seacombe cliffs with Winspit and lynchets in the background.

Acton Quarries (SY 990 783): The Trust owns a series of open-cast stone quarries around the hamlet of Acton to the west of Langton Matravers. Some date back to the eighteenth century. Though the bulk of the modern output has been for aggregates, for road-making, rather than building stone, the Trust's own crop of character cottages generates a continuing demand for roofing slates and the better class of restorations. Generally, the currently more restrained architectural climate is reviving the use of shaped blocks of cut stone.

The Trust intends to restore much of the worked-out land to agriculture but disused quarries are being preserved for their industrial, archaeological and conservation interest. Abandoned underground workings provide nationally important bat roosts that are leased to the Dorset Trust for Nature Conservation.

Landscape: There is still downland turf on these central stone cliffs of southern Purbeck and the slopes of its limestone plateau. On top there are arable fields north of Eastington Farm and Sea Spray but the rough pastures extend inland up the coombes. The Trust's holding stretches to Abbascombe and Eastington Farm, and to the present-day quarrylands west of Acton.

Trust ownership: 850 acres, part of the Corfe Castle Estate bequeathed by Ralph Bankes in 1982.

Seacombe's quarries and (opposite) its cliffs, looking east.

Location and access: Crossed by the coastal footpath from St Alban's Head to Durlston Head, but the most direct paths are from Worth Matravers [turn eastwards from just below the pond and cross the first ridge of hills into the next valley, then turn right, down the valley to Seacombe] which is a mile away.

Alternatively you can approach from the Swanage side. Park near Langton Matravers School and take the path via Dancing Ledge to the coastal footpath. Turn right, westwards, along the coast path. You come first to Hedbury and then descend to Seacombe. Hedbury is a mile and a half away from Langton Matravers and Seacombe two miles.

STUDLAND HEATH NATIONAL NATURE RESERVE including GODLINGSTON HEATH, THE AGGLESTONE, PUCKSTONE, LITTLE SEA, SHELL BAY, THE TRAINING BANK, BRAMBLE BUSH BAY and REDHORN QUAY
north and west of Studland   *SZ 020 830*

Geology: Outcrops of dark-red iron-impregnated sandstone of the Bagshot beds, the eroded remains of a layer of rock that once covered the sands and clays of the heath. The notable stone is the Agglestone, which is sixteen feet high, twice that in diameter, and weighs four hundred tons. It was one of the natural

The Agglestone, from the west.

wonders of Purbeck, but the famous mushroom-shape was lost in September 1970 when it collapsed on its side.

Legend: The Agglestone was thrown by the Devil at Corfe Castle, from the Isle of Wight – but fell short.

Names: 'Agglestone' means 'hailstone', the belief being it came from the sky. Puckstone, to the north-west, is also romantic; puck being a goblin.

Landforms: The great sandy beaches of Studland and Shell Bay grow into wide dunes that enclose on the South Haven Peninsula [east of the Ferry Road] a remarkable freshwater lagoon, the Little Sea.

Little Sea   (SZ 030 845):   Dating from 1700 to 1850, before that being an arm of the open sea.   Dune build-up cut off its tidal channel, which was the outlet from the north-east of the lake, and created a freshwater lagoon.   The channel can still be traced as alternating patches of marshland and carr scrub.   When the Ordnance Survey re-surveyed the beach east of Little Sea in 1959 they found the high water mark had jumped fifty yards out to sea in only five years.   Eels are common in Little Sea and rarely it has otters.   The frequent visitors are heron, fishing for palmate newts.   Dabchick are also there in the summer, being the only grebes to breed in Purbeck, but it is winter when it attracts flocks of waterfowl.   These include garganey, gadwall, goldeneye, common scoter, scaup, mute swan and whooper swan. Redpoll breed in the surrounding birch clumps.

The Agglestone, from the north.

Godlingston Heath: northwards, to Poole Harbour and Brownsea Island.

Godlingston Heath: the Puckstone from the south-east.

The landlocked Little Sea.

Bronze Age burial mounds (SZ 006 820, SZ 018 822 and SZ 018 827): Scattered groupings of round barrows along the southern fringes of the heath. Four are at the south-western extremity of Godlingston Heath, in the field that is reverting to gorseland east of Kingswood Farm, between the viewpoint layby and the golf course. Three of these mounds are bell barrows, rather than the common bowl type, the difference being an area of untouched flat ground between the mound and its ditch. They are up to four feet high. Thorny Barrow, Fishing Barrow [so named for its waterlogged ditch] and three other mounds are on the central southern part of the heath near the golf course. Fishing Barrow has suffered the indignity of being flattened at the top for a golf tee. All are burial mounds of the rich Wessex culture established by warrior Beaker folk who immigrated from the Rhine, and are dated between 2,100 and 1,500 BC.

Salt pans (SZ 026 857): Between Jerry's Point and Redhorn Quay, on the Poole Harbour shore towards Brand's Bay, there are seventy-one salt-pans and another six between Brand's Ford and Greenland. Each is a depression about twenty feet across, slightly dished and surrounded by a circular bank about a foot high. There is no evidence to suggest their date but they are probably either Roman or mediaeval. One group has an associated batch of sandy mounds.

High-water at the north end of Studland Bay: with the Training Bank under it (centre) as a lighter line from left to right. Beyond the Swash Channel is the high-rise skyline of clifftop Bournemouth.

Boundary or other stones (SZ 027 852): Six stones, now fallen, are in a line along the centre of the South Haven Peninsula, near the site of the demolished Curlew Cottages to the east of the Ferry Road. Their function is unknown.

Bramble Bush Bay (SZ 030 860): The inlet southwards from Gravel Point on the harbour side of the South Haven Peninsula has had moorings for houseboats since before the Great War.

Redhorn Quay (SZ 021 855): Disused ancient jetty at the north-east corner of Brand's Bay, the traditional crossing point from Poole to the South Haven Peninsula before the road was opened to its northern tip – which was only a narrow spit in mediaeval times. Old blocks of granite, however, are not part of any jetty. They seem to have been ballast dumped by Cornish craft.

Stone and clay-pits (SZ 015 827): The central parts of Godlingston Heath were dug in the Middle Ages and until the nineteenth century for the brown gritstone or carr-stone, now more generally called heathstone, which can be seen in many of the farm buildings to the north of Purbeck Hills. It is often mixed with grey Purbeck stone in some of the grander buildings of east Dorset, including Wimborne Minster. There are traces of claypits in the north-west corner of the heath, the boundary of which is now the conifer plantations of the Rempstone Estate.

The village end of Studland Bay: Redend Point is tree-smothered at the right, concealing Fort Henry.

The Training Bank (SZ 041 861 to SZ 048 851): From the east side of Shell Bay a man-made spit of rocks can be followed for more than half a mile into Poole Harbour at low tide. This was constructed in the 1930s and holds the sands back from the Swash Channel approach to the harbour entrance.

Landscape: The interesting ecology of the heath is not on the conspicuous drier crests but in the pockets of acid bog. Here amongst the sphagnum grow highly specialised species. *Erica ciliaris* is the "Dorset Heath", and grows only in Purbeck and the Pyrenees. It thrives here with the blue marsh gentian, insectivorous sundews, tufts of cotton grass, and the burnt orchid. Look out for colourful dragonflies, and green woodpeckers ("yaffles" these are called in Dorset) which fly out of the sallow scrub fringing the heath. The sandier parts are mainly notable for the smooth snake (*Coronella austriaca*) and its sand lizard prey (*Lacerta agilis agilis*) which are now on the point of extinction from most other areas of their specialised heathland habitat. Ironically the first British record for the smooth snake came in 1859 from what is now the Bournemouth International Centre. Though harmless it was common enough to be killed there in scores in the 1868 drought. It is now fully protected by law. Stonechats nest in the dense old heather. The cocky purple-breasted Dartford warbler prefers the gorse scrub, or "vurze" as it is in the Dorset tongue. The changing fortunes of this bird and these wild lands are described in my book on *Purbeck's Heath* [1987].

Studland: inter-tidal companionship and play.

Studland: sand dunes between storms.

Trust ownership: 2,500 acres, 1,500 of which are leased to the Nature Conservancy for a National Nature Reserve. This was established in 1962 and extended later. Part of the Corfe Castle Estate left to the Trust by Ralph Bankes in 1982.

Location and access: Studland is approached from Corfe Castle by the B3351 or from the north, across the mouth of Poole Harbour, by a pay-ferry from Sandbanks at Poole. There are large beach car-parks at Studland; the Knoll car-park has the capacity for 1,700 cars. There is also parking at Shell Bay and in a viewpoint layby beside the B3351 a short distance west of the Golf Course.

Public paths lead across the heath from the east side of the Golf Course. The western one is to the north-west corner of Godlingston Heath. The centre one crosses the middle of the heath. The eastern one goes to Studland with an offshoot to the Agglestone, one mile.

The Agglestone can also be reached from Studland, west from the start of the Ferry Road between Studland Bay House and the Knoll House Hotel.

Coastal paths follow the edge of the dunes and run close to the shores of Poole Harbour. This is the busiest place in Dorset at the height of the summer, with all the car parks filling early and at some weekends police road-blocks to prevent any more visitors approaching from Corfe Castle.

It is a nature reserve with some human naturists in the warmer weather. The Trust's 1986 management plan comments: "The use of the central section of Studland Bay by nudists will be accepted but every effort made through an increased wardening presence to persuade naturists to remain within accepted boundaries on the beach.   Regular liaison will be maintained with the Police."

STUDLAND VILLAGE, SAXON CROSS-BASE, STUDLAND MANOR HOTEL, BANKES ARMS HOTEL and CLIFF END
north of Swanage   *SZ 035 824*

Studland village: Though surrounded by the Bankes estate the parish church had remained in the advowson – patronage, being the right to appoint the rector – of the Pleydell family since the seventeenth century.   Despite that the church inevitably has strong Bankes connections and the items that follow mention some of these.

   St. Nicholas's church is enthusiastically described by Fred Pitfield in his *Purbeck Parish Churches* [1985] as "the oldest surviving complete church in Dorset".   Its Saxon origins and the quality and extent of the Norman work show that Studland started life as a place of some importance.   Fortunately, for the survival of the church, it was to stay a village.   In other places the churches

Studland: options. To the village; 'Church Only'; or the beach.

expanded with the population but in Studland "its ancient church has survived practically in its original state".   Note the magnificent mid–twelfth century internal tower arch and the south doorway.   There are also Norman windows, bowl–shaped font, corbel–table heads, and moulded capitals.   An unexpected early treasure is a Coptic processional cross from sixth century Egypt though that has come as a gift from a parishioner.   The inscription is partly decipherable: "This is the cross of... Blessed be his seed.   Who gave it to Mary, the daughter of..."

Romano–British stone–lined graves have been found in the churchyard, including that of a decapitated woman.   She was dug up in 1951 and now resides in the Red House Museum, Christchurch.   Her head had been taken off after death; probably in the belief that this would still a restless spirit.

Studland therefore shows the conversion of a pagan sacred site into that for a Christian Saxon church.

Memorials to Cornet Bankes VC: A stained glass window in Studland church and an inscription on the Bankes family tomb in the churchyard record the heroism of Cornet Bankes.   He was the son of the late George Bankes MP of Kingston Lacy but his memorials are here because he preferred the Studland end of the estate and had a passion for sailing.

Cornet Bankes was killed during the Indian Mutiny.   He went to India in

Studland: 'Church Only' – the oldest complete church in Dorset.

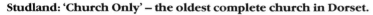

1857, at the age of twenty-one, as a subaltern in the 7th Hussars. The Times correspondent, William Howard Russell, would tell the world of his courage in repelling a rebel charge at the end of the British siege of their stronghold at Lucknow, on 19 March 1858:

"A band of Ghazees, who issued out of an old mud fort and charged the guns and the party of the 7th Hussars covering them, had got the lad down and hacked at him in that cruel way until he was rescued by his comrades. It is perfectly astonishing, to witness his cheerfulness and resignation."

"If I get out of this, Russell," the fatally wounded young man said, "They tell me I'll be able to go yachting, and that's all I care about. We'll have many a jolly cruise together." He paused for a moment: "If it please God."

Cornet Bankes was dying in the hospital of the 53rd Regiment in the Indian Imam Bara temple-palace at Lucknow. Russell described his injuries as frightful:

"One leg lopped off above the knee, one arm cut off, the other leg nearly severed, the other arm cut through the bone, and several cuts on the body."

Whilst lying there he heard that Sir Colin Campbell had recommended him for the Victoria Cross. It would be confirmed by the Queen and given to his mother at Kingston Lacy. Cornet Bankes died on 6 April 1858 and was buried in the churchyard of the ruined cantonment church that stood close to the camp of the 7th Hussars.

Gravestone of Sergeant William Lawrence: A stone in the churchyard at Studland sets out the graphic military career of Waterloo veteran Sergeant William Lawrence who retired from the 40th Regiment of Foot to keep the Duke of Wellington public house [now the Bankes Arms Hotel] and died at the age of seventy-eight:

"To the honoured memory of Serjeant William Lawrence (of the 40th Regiment Foot) who after a long and eventful life in the service of his country peacefully ended his days at Studland November 11th 1869. He served with his distinguished regiment in the war in South America 1805 and through the whole of the Peninsular War 1808-1813. He received a silver medal and no less than ten clasps for the battles in which he was engaged – Roleia, Vimiera, Talavera, Ciudad Rodrigo, Badajoz (in which desperate assault being one of the volunteers for the forlorn hope he was most severely wounded), Vittoria, Pyrenees, Nivells, Orthes, Toulouse. He also fought at the glorious victory of Waterloo June 18th 1815.

"While still serving with his Regiment during the Occupation of Paris by the Allied Armies Serjeant Lawrence married Clotilde Clairet at St. Germain-en-Laye who died Septr. 26th 1853 and was buried beneath this Spot."

They have one of the best biographical gravestones in Europe.

Saxon cross-base (SZ 036 824): The heathstone block, four feet in diameter, at the base of the 1970s Celtic-style cross beside the lane leading to the church is the only surviving part of a mediaeval preaching cross in the Isle of Purbeck. Its modern Purbeck stone top has Saxon type scroll work though it incorporates clues to its date – such as a Concorde airliner.

Studland Manor Hotel (SZ 037 827): The estate's marine villa, which was built by George Bankes MP [died 1856] and used by his sons, including Cornet who is mentioned above, as the base for their sailing adventures into the Channel. It may incorporate earlier walls. The general contrived irregularity includes two round towers, on the north-west side, which may have been inspired by the lost Studland Castle at Old Harry Rocks. Inside, the building has re-used fittings such as a Gothic landing, a fine eighteenth century carved fireplace, and a door surround featuring Orpheus in the forest with the wild animals.

Bankes Arms Hotel (SZ 037 825): Formerly the Duke of Wellington and then the New Inn. A modern re-building of the stone-roofed cottage that used to form a rustic setting on the back lane just above the little chine that opens on to Studland's offshoot beach, the one south-east of Redend Point. From the 1820s to the 1850s, as the Duke of Wellington, it was kept by William Lawrence, the Waterloo veteran whose exploits are set out above.

Cliff End (SZ 038 825): Here a promising 38-year-old mathematician named Bertrand Russell first went to bed with Lady Ottoline Morrell, the wife of Liberal MP Philip Morrell, during the Easter of 1911. The affair lasted until 1916 when Russell was thrown out of Trinity College for his opposition to the Great War. Bertrand became the third Earl Russell in 1931, on the death of his elder brother, and is remembered as an anti-nuclear campaigner and a philosopher. His Studland interlude was spent at Cliff End, a house in the trees between the Bankes Arms Hotel and the small beach that lies to the south-east of Redend Point.

Landscape: Studland is a scattering of cottages and later houses on a wooded rise between three hundred and a thousand yards inland from Redend Point at the south-west corner of Studland Bay. The village and its paddocks are fringed on the northern side by heathland, to the east by sandy cliffs fifty feet or so in height, and on the southern extremity by rolling chalk cereal lands.

Trust ownership: 500 acres, part of the Corfe Castle Estate left to the Trust by Ralph Bankes in 1982.

Location and access: Use the beach car-parks, off the B3351 – the road from Corfe Castle – rather than try to park in the narrow lanes. Get there early if you are coming on a hot day at the height of the summer.

VERNEY FARM
south of Swanage   *SZ 009 779*

Landscape: Part of the limestone plateau of southern Purbeck, immediately west of the old Swanage quarrylands at the Langton Matravers end of the parish. Sloping coastal grasslands, rising to 400 feet and rich in orchids and other wild flowers, at the top of sheer stone cliffs a hundred feet high.

Trust ownership: 150 acres, part of the Corfe Castle Estate bequeathed by Ralph Bankes in 1982.

Location and access: A mile and a quarter walk along the cliff path, west from the Dorset County Council's car-park in the Durlston Country Park. You turn south along Swanage seafront for almost as far as you can go. Turn right near the end, up Seymer Road, and then continue uphill into Durlston Road.

The car-park is at the end. You walk westwards along the coastal path, with your back to the Anvil Point lighthouse, and walk the length of the Country Park to a stile in an old stone wall. Next come the three fields of the National Trust's Belle Vue cliffs (which have their own entry) and then after one more, narrower field, you cross the boundary into the Verney Farm clifftop.

Together these three public access properties have created a general freedom for you to roam over all but one field of the south-eastern corner of the Isle of Purbeck.

Verney Farm: Langton Matravers behind with Corfe Castle in the middle distance.

WHITECLIFF FARM, BALLARD DOWN and PUNFIELD COVE
north of Swanage   *SZ 030 810*

Punfield cove (SZ 040 810): The dip in the undercliff at the Swanage end of the chalk on Ballard Cliff [not named by the Ordnance Survey, but known locally as Punfield] is of considerable geological interest. It is highly fossiliferous and contains the Punfield marine band which has Spanish affinities. This lies in the cretaceous layers, of the final Mesozoic period, when the lower greensand and colourful Wealden sands were accumulating in the warm waters.

Whitecliff Farm: westward to the Trust's Godlingston Hill.

Bronze Age burial mounds (SZ 040 813):   There are eight skyline round barrows on Ballard Down, which were raised to cover aristocratic burials about 1,800 BC.   Three were opened by John Austen in 1851 and he returned to do another trio in 1857.   The hollows at the centre of the mounds are his mark.

Underneath he found crouched skeletons, with one such primary burial under each mound, and pieces of antler-pick which had been used to quarry the chalk.   Later Bronze Age burials had been inserted in some of the mounds, in the form of cremations, and from these Austen found urn fragments.   There was also the burial of a child in a pit that had been cut into the chalk.

Several of the mounds were damaged by Second World War defences, apparently for a radar apparatus, and they have been subsequently virtually levelled by ploughing.

Strip lynchets (SZ 028 807):   Three mediaeval raised strip fields survive in a poor condition north-west of Whitecliff Farm, and this open field formerly extended to the foot of Ballard Down.   There was a Saxon settlement at Whitecliff, listed by the Normans in their Domesday Survey of 1086.

Boundary stones (westwards from SZ 040 813):   Eight eighteenth century boundary stones, along the fenceline of Ballard Down, mark the limits of "SM" [Swanage Manor] and the parish of Studland.   The second stone from the east, 250 yards west from the main cluster of barrows, is dated 1776.

Punfield, Ballard Point, and Swanage Bay.

Landscape: The 500 feet high chalk spine of Ballard Down stretches for well over a mile and has fine views in all directions.

Southwards the view is over the Swanage valley and northwards it is across the heath and harbour to Poole and Bournemouth. Seawards the panorama brings in Studland Bay, the cliffs to the entrance of The Solent, and then the whole western side of the Isle of Wight from The Needles to St Catherine's Point.

The south-facing chalk escarpments have a disappointing flora as the extremes of heat and dryness are too much for most herbs.

Trust ownership: 222 acres, bought with Enterprise Neptune appeal funds in 1976.

Location and access: There are public footpaths to Whitecliff Farm and Punfield [the latter being beside the coastal footpath] from Hill Road and Ballard Road at the northern edge of Swanage.

Alternatively you can park in the large layby beside the mosaic of glazed tiles that depict "Swanage" on the Swanage-Studland road at the south side of the Ulwell Gap. From here you follow the public path notices, around the reservoir, to the top of Ballard Down. There is a path down to Whitecliff Farm, on the south side in about half a mile, and another to Punfield Cove in a further half mile.

Ballard Down and Ballard Point: from Swanage beach.

WILKSWOOD FARM, TALBOT'S WOOD, LANGTON WEST WOOD, THE WILDERNESS, GODLINGSTON WOOD, WOODHOUSE HILL and other PURBECK AMENITY WOODLAND

principally to the north of Langton Matravers, with other woodlands at Godlingston and Studland   *SY 996 796*

Roman buildings at Woodhouse Hill (SZ 031 822): These are just inside the eastern boundary of the woods to the south-west of Studland, above the B3351 road as it reaches the edge of the village. Apparently they comprised a forge or small manufactory which was in use from about 65 to 85 AD. An excavation was carried out by Norman Field in 1952-58. He found a rectangular hut with a clay-built shelf on which rested a high-class Samian platter, imported from southern Gaul, a circa 73 AD coin of the Emperor Vespasian [the conqueror of Hod Hill three decades earlier] and a brooch. Nearby huts had pieces of crucibles which were used for copper or bronze working. Iron slag was a further indication that metal was worked on the site.

Another group of finds showed resumed occupation in the third and early fourth centuries.

Wilkswood Quarries (SY 994 795): The Trust's woodlands in the valley north of Langton Matravers, on the slopes to the south of the stream, conceal thirteenth century marble workings which provided building stone for cathedrals and effigies for the distinguished dead of much of Britain. Some of the stone was exported to Ireland and the continent.

It is not a true marble but a vein of highly fossiliferous freshwater limestone that cuts smooth and takes a polish. The sites of the workings and their sledge tracks are beneath an eerie tangle of undergrowth in the valley, from Wilkswood Farm through Langton West Wood and westward towards Primrose Hill.

Landscape: The main belt of ancient deciduous woodland in the Isle of Purbeck is on the Trust's lands around Wilkswood Farm. It includes Langton West Wood to the west, and The Wilderness to the north beside the railway line.

Godlingston Wood is another patch of older woodland, on the spring-line to the north of the ancient manor house [*see its entry*].

Woodhouse Hill at Studland is also elderly remnant tree-cover, on a spur of sandstone at the 200 feet contour between the main heath and the open, rolling chalklands on the north slopes of Ballard Down. The Trust also owns the other small woods around Studland but these are mainly recent plantations.

Trust ownership: 254 acres of amenity woodland were part of the Corfe Castle Estate left to the Trust by Ralph Bankes in 1982.

Location and access: The principal batch of ancient woodlands, to the north of Langton Matravers, are reached from the lane on the north side of the B3069 a hundred yards west from the village schools. This becomes a path in a third of a mile, after the last buildings, and tracks branch off to the left towards Primrose Hill and to the right to Talbot's Wood. If you continue straight ahead, for another third of a mile, you come to the valley bottom and cross the stream. Then, in a hundred yards, you cross another public highway. This is a bridleway which to the left skirts Langton West Wood and leads to Quarr [the Dorset dialect word for the business].

To the right the bridleway runs along the northern side of the valley above Wilkswood Farm. The alternative is to continue straight ahead, for a quarter of a mile, to the small but aptly named woodland, The Wilderness, overlooking the cutting of the dismantled railway [in 1986 restoration work had reached New Barn, half a mile to the east, as the Swanage Railway rebuilt its way out of the town].

Godlingston Wood (SZ 015 805) is beside a public path that runs northwards from the track that branches off the lane, on the north side, between the cemetery and Godlingston Manor. There is a small lake at the south end of the woods. These then extend around a semi-circular coombe at the foot of the Purbeck Hills.

Woodhouse Hill (SZ 030 823) lies on the north side of the main road into Studland, 250 yards from the edge of the village. The villa or workshops, some slight walls of which remain, is seventy yards up the slope near the eastern boundary of the wood.

THE RATINGS
Dorset's top three

The top three Dorset properties in 1986 were:

1 *Corfe Castle* – with 154,500 visitors
2 *Brownsea Island* – with 110,500 visitors
3 *Kingston Lacy* – with 108,500 visitors (its first full year)

As for the open space popularity stakes it is impossible to hold a fair contest because most of the car-parks are uncontrolled.   The following league table is therefore purely a personal estimate of how the public seemed to be voting with its wheels:

1 *Studland Beach*
2 *Badbury Rings*
3 *Seatown Beach*
4 *The Hardy Monument*
5 *Stonebarrow Hill*
6 *Langdon Hill*

Appendix

NATIONAL TRUST DORSET –
some of its TREASURES IN LONDON

'The Bankes Leaf'
in the British Library

One of history's lost pages came to light in 1984 among the Bankes estate papers in the boot room at Kingston Lacy House.   It was a vellum leaf which had been re-used as the wrapping for a 1585 copy of a Purbeck title deed.   This, it transpired, had come from one of the most famous of the pre-Conquest great bibles, assembled on the instructions of the Venerable Bede in about 712.   Bede records in his *History of the Holy Abbots* how he told Ceolfrith to make three such manuscript copies of the bible, one each for his monasteries of Jarrow and Wearmouth – and the third for the Pope.

That copy went with Ceolfrith to Rome in 716, but the abbot died in France and his bible later came into the possession of the monastery of Monte Amiata, near Florence.   It was put in the Laurentian Library in that city in 1786 and is known as the *Codex Amiatinus*.

The two Wearside bibles were considered to be completely lost but in 1909 Canon Greenwell of Durham came across a leaf in a junk shop in Newcastle.   His discovery enabled eleven more leaves to be found, re-used as bindings in the muniments at Wollaton Hall, Nottinghamshire. These were acquired by the British Museum in the 1930s.

One of Ceolfrith's Wearside bibles was stripped apart at Wollaton in the early 1580s, being used for their vellum as folders for copies of title deeds and other legal documents. These transcripts were made in 1585 when Sir Christopher Hatton bought the Wollaton estate from Francis Willoughby.

Hatton, a favourite of Elizabeth I, sat in Parliament for Northamptonshire, though he was losing the queen's attentions in 1584. She had given him Corfe Castle in 1575 and the page from the bible – now known as the Bankes Leaf – was used to bind one of the copies of the deeds relating to the Purbeck estate. By 1585 Hatton was Elizabeth's key man along all four sides of the square that cornered Elizabeth, Parliament, Mary Queen of Scots and the courts. In 1585, Hatton was rewarded with Northamptonshire lands, acquired Wollaton in Nottingham, and was given the keepership of the royal hunting forest of the Isle of Purbeck.

The page from Ceolfrith's bible was spotted in that neglected deed box at Kingston Lacy by Nicholas Pickwoad, the National Trust's consultant on book conservation, who passed it to John Fuggles, the Trust's libraries adviser. Both realised it was important, though at that time neither realised that they were handling pre-Conquest parchment. The Trust then decided it was of such national significance that it should be kept in the British Library.

Badbury area
Bronze Age finds
in the British Museum

The displays of British prehistory in the British Museum galleries include Bronze Age urns and food vessels from Straw Barrow and its neighbouring mounds near Badbury Rings. The 1845 excavators also removed a sandstone block carved with daggers and axes.

Hod Hill exhibits
in the British Museum

The Romano-British displays in the British Museum include the major finds from Hod Hill. The material includes the Victorian collection of antiquities from Hod gathered together by Henry Durden of Blandford. In 1951-57 the British Museum carried out its own excavations of the Roman Fort in the north-west corner of the Iron Age hill-fort. The finds include spearheads and ballista-bolts, a bronze oil lamp, tinned buckles and a pendant which are inlaid with niello, and brooches.

Index